ARK PAPERBACKS

DICTIONARY OF ANALYTICAL PSYCHOLOGY

'Jung is a thinker who has affected us so deeply that many of his ideas have passed into common currency, and few people remember who was their originator.' – Philip Toynbee, *Observer*

A general description of psychological types, this dictionary sums up Jung's ideas and provides a valuable introduction for anyone who wants to understand Jung's typology and his ideas about the human personality. Jung believed that it is one's psychological type which from the outset determines and limits a person's judgment, so that his system of types is of central importance in his work.

Based on Jung's years of practical experience as a doctor and practising psychotherapist, the dictionary is a thoroughly practical work, rich in insights into the relation of the individual to the world, to people and to things.

C. G. JUNG

C. G. Jung (1875-1961), the Swiss psychiatrist and founder of Analytical Psychology, was an original thinker who made an immense contribution to the understanding of the human mind. In his early years he was a lecturer in psychiatry at the University of Zürich and collaborated with Sigmund Freud. He gave up teaching to devote himself to his private practice in psychiatry and to research. He travelled widely and was a prolific author, often writing on subjects other than analytical psychology, such as mythology, alchemy, flying saucers and the problem of time. Jung was also responsible for defining such influential and widely-used terms as the Collective Unconscious, Extraversion/Introversion and Archetypes.

ARK PAPERBACKS is an imprint of Routledge & Kegan Paul and can be ordered through your usual bookshop.

ARK

C.G.JUNG
DICTIONARY OF ANALYTICAL PSYCHOLOGY

ARK PAPERBACKS
London and New York

This edition first published in Great Britain in 1987 by ARK
Extracted from Psychological Types, Vol. 6, of
The Collected Works of C.G. Jung, edited by
Herbert Read, Michael Fordham and Gerhard Adler

ARK PAPERBACKS is an imprint of
Routledge & Kegan Paul Ltd
11 New Fetter Lane, London EC4P 4EE

Printed in Great Britain by
Cox and Wyman Ltd, Reading

ISBN 0–7448–0077–3

CONTENTS

GENERAL DESCRIPTION OF THE TYPES

1. INTRODUCTION

In the following pages I shall attempt a general description of the psychology of the types, starting with the two basic types I have termed introverted and extraverted. This will be followed by a description of those more special types whose peculiarities are due to the fact that the individual adapts and orients himself chiefly by means of his most differentiated function. The former I would call *attitude-types*, distinguished by the direction of their interest, or of the movement of libido; the latter I would call *function-types*.

The attitude-types, as I have repeatedly emphasized in the preceding chapters, are distinguished by their attitude to the object. The introvert's attitude is an abstracting one; at bottom, he is always intent on withdrawing libido from the object, as though he had to prevent the object from gaining power over him. The extravert, on the contrary, has a positive relation to the object. He affirms its importance to such an extent that his subjective attitude is constantly related to and oriented by the object. The object can never have enough value for him, and its importance must always be increased. The two types are so different and present such a striking contrast that their existence becomes quite obvious even to the layman once it has been pointed out. Everyone knows those reserved, inscrutable, rather shy people who form the strongest possible contrast to the open, sociable, jovial, or at least friendly and approachable characters who are on good terms with everybody, or quarrel with everybody, but always relate to them in some way and in turn are affected by them.

One is naturally inclined, at first, to regard such differences as mere idiosyncrasies of character peculiar to individuals. But anyone with a thorough knowledge of human nature will soon discover that the contrast is by no means a matter of isolated individual instances but of typical attitudes which are far more common than one with limited psychological experience would assume. Indeed, as the preceding chapters may have shown, it is a fundamental contrast, sometimes quite clear, sometimes obscured, but always apparent when one is dealing with individuals whose personality is in any way pronounced. Such people are found not merely among the educated, but in all ranks of society, so that our types can be discovered among labourers and peasants no less than among the most highly differentiated members of a community. Sex makes no difference either; one finds the same contrast among women of all classes. Such a widespread distribution could hardly have come about if it were merely a question of a conscious and deliberate choice of attitude. In that case, one would surely find one particular attitude in one particular class of people linked together by a common education and background and localized accordingly. But that is not so at all; on the contrary, the types seem to be distributed quite at random. In the same family one child is introverted, the other extraverted. Since the facts show that the attitude-type is a general phenomenon having an apparently random distribution, it cannot be a matter of conscious judgment or conscious intention, but must be due to some unconscious, instinctive cause. As a general psychological phenomenon, therefore, the type antithesis must have some kind of biological foundation.

The relation between subject and object, biologically considered, is always one of adaptation, since every relation between subject and object presupposes the modification of one by the other through reciprocal influence. Adaptation consists in these constant modifications. The typical attitudes to the object, therefore, are processes of adaptation. There are in nature two fundamentally different modes of adaptation which ensure the continued existence of the living organism. The one consists in a high rate of fertility, with low powers of defence and short duration of life for the single individual; the other consists in equipping the individual with numerous means of self-preservation plus a low fertility rate. This biological difference, it seems to me, is not merely analogous to, but the actual foundation of, our two psychological modes of adaptation. I must content myself with this broad hint. It is sufficient to note that the peculiar nature of the extravert constantly urges him to expend and propagate himself in every way, while the tendency of the introvert is to defend himself against all demands from outside, to conserve his energy by withdrawing it from objects, thereby consolidating his own position. Blake's intuition did not err when he described the two classes of men as "prolific" and "devouring."[1] Just as, biologically, the two modes of adaptation work equally well and are successful in their own way, so too with the typical attitudes. The one achieves its end by a multiplicity of relationships, the other by monopoly.

The fact that children often exhibit a typical attitude quite unmistakably even in their earliest years forces us to assume that it cannot be the struggle for existence in the ordinary sense that determines a particular attitude. It might be objected, cogently enough, that even the infant at the breast has to perform an unconscious act of psychological adaptation, in that the mother's influence leads to specific reactions in the child. This argument, while supported by incontestable evidence, becomes rather flimsy in face of the equally incontestable fact that two children of the same mother may exhibit contrary attitudes at an early age, though no change in the mother's attitude can be demonstrated. Although nothing would induce me to underrate the incalculable importance of parental influence, this familiar experience compels me to conclude that the decisive factor must be looked for in the disposition of the child. Ultimately, it must be the individual disposition which decides whether the child will belong to this or that type despite the constancy of external conditions. Naturally I am thinking only of normal cases. Under abnormal conditions, i.e., when the mother's own attitude is extreme, a similar attitude can be forced on the children too, thus violating their individual disposition, which might have opted for another type if no abnormal external influences had intervened. As a rule, whenever such a falsification of type takes place as a result of parental influence, the individual becomes neurotic later, and can be cured only by developing the attitude consonant with his nature.

[1] See *Psychological Types*, par. 460.

As to the individual disposition, I have nothing to say except that there are obviously individuals who have a greater capacity, or to whom it is more congenial, to adapt in one way and not in another. It may well be that physiological causes of which we have no knowledge play a part in this. I do not think it improbable, in view of one's experience that a reversal of type often proves exceedingly harmful to the physiological well-being of the organism, usually causing acute exhaustion.

2. THE EXTRAVERTED TYPE

In our description of this and the following types it is necessary, for the sake of clarity, to distinguish between the psychology of consciousness and the psychology of the unconscious. We shall first describe the phenomena of consciousness.

a. The General Attitude of Consciousness

Although it is true that everyone orients himself in accordance with the data supplied by the outside world, we see every day that the data in themselves are only relatively decisive. The fact that it is cold outside prompts one man to put on his overcoat, while another, who wants to get hardened, finds this superfluous. One man admires the latest tenor because everybody else does, another refuses to do so, not because he dislikes him, but because in his view the subject of universal admiration is far from having been proved admirable. One man resigns himself to circumstances because experience has shown him that nothing else is possible, another is convinced that though things have gone the same way a thousand times before, the thousand and first time will be different. The one allows himself to be oriented by the given facts, the other holds in reserve a view which interposes itself between him and the objective data. Now, when orientation by the object predominates in such a way that decisions and actions are determined not by subjective views but by objective conditions, we speak of an extraverted attitude. When this is habitual, we speak of an extraverted type. If a man thinks, feels, acts, and actually lives in a way that is *directly* correlated with the objective conditions and their demands, he is extraverted. His life makes it

4

perfectly clear that it is the object and not this subjective view that plays the determining role in his consciousness. Naturally he has subjective views too, but their determining value is less than that of the objective conditions. Consequently, he never expects to find any absolute factors in his own inner life, since the only ones he knows are outside himself. Like Epimetheus, his inner life is subordinated to external necessity, though not without a struggle; but it is always the objective determinant that wins in the end. His whole consciousness looks outward, because the essential and decisive determination always comes from outside. But it comes from outside only because that is where he expects it to come from. All the peculiarities of his psychology, except those that depend on the primacy of one particular psychological function or on idiosyncrasies of character, follow from this basic attitude. His interest and attention are directed to objective happenings, particularly those in his immediate environment. Not only people but things seize and rivet his attention. Accordingly, they also determine his actions, which are fully explicable on those grounds. The actions of the extravert are recognizably related to external conditions. In so far as they are not merely reactive to environmental stimuli, they have a character that is always adapted to the actual circumstances, and they find sufficient play within the limits of the objective situation. No serious effort is made to transcend these bounds. It is the same with his interest: objective happenings have an almost inexhaustible fascination for him, so that ordinarily he never looks for anything else.

The moral laws governing his actions coincide with the demands of society, that is, with the prevailing moral standpoint. If this were to change, the extravert's subjective moral guidelines would change accordingly, without this altering his general psychological habits in any way. This strict determination by objective factors does not mean, as one might suppose, a complete let alone ideal adaptation to the general conditions of life. In the eyes of the extravert, of course, an *adjustment* of this kind to the objective situation must seem like complete adaptation, since for him no other criterion exists. But from a higher point of view it by no means follows that the objective situation is in all circumstances a normal one. It can quite well be temporarily or locally abnormal. An individual who adjusts himself to it is admittedly conforming to the style of his environment, but together with his whole surroundings he is in an abnormal situation with respect to the universally valid laws of life. He may indeed thrive in such surroundings, but only up to the point where he and his milieu meet with disaster for transgressing these laws. He will share the general collapse to exactly the same extent as he was adjusted to the previous situation. Adjustment is not adaptation; adaptation requires far more than merely going along smoothly with the conditions of the moment. (Once again I would remind the reader of Spitteler's Epimetheus.) It requires observance of laws more universal than the immediate conditions of time and place. The very adjustment of the normal extraverted type is his limitation. He owes his normality on the one hand to his ability to fit into existing conditions with comparative ease. His requirements are limited to the objectively possible, for instance to the career that holds out good prospects at this particular moment; he does what is needed of him, or what is expected of him, and refrains from all innovations that are not entirely self-evident or that in any way exceed the expectations of those around him. On the other hand, his normality must also depend essentially on whether he takes account of his subjective needs and requirements, and this is just his weak point, for the tendency of his type is so outer-directed that even the most obvious of all subjective facts, the condition of his own body, receives scant attention. The body is not sufficiently objective or "outside," so that the satisfaction of elementary needs which are indispensable to physical well-being is no longer given its due. The body accordingly suffers, to say nothing of the psyche. The extravert is usually unaware of this latter fact, but it is all the more apparent to his household. He feels his loss of equilibrium only when it announces itself in abnormal body sensations. These he cannot ignore. It is quite natural that he should regard them as concrete and "objective," since with his type of mentality they cannot be anything else—for him. In others he at once sees "imagination" at work. A too extraverted attitude can also become so oblivious of the subject that the latter is sacrificed completely to so-called objective demands—to the demands, for instance, of a continually expanding business, because orders are piling up and profitable opportunities have to be exploited.

This is the extravert's danger: he gets sucked into objects and completely loses himself in them. The resultant functional disorders, nervous or physical, have a compensatory value, as they force him into an involuntary self-restraint. Should the symptoms be functional, their peculiar character may express his psychological situation in symbolic form; for instance, a singer whose fame has risen to dangerous heights that tempt him to expend too much energy suddenly finds he cannot sing high notes because of some nervous inhibition. Or a man of modest beginnings who rapidly reaches a social position of great influence with wide prospects is suddenly afflicted with all the symptoms of a mountain sickness.[2] Again, a man about to marry a woman of doubtful character whom he adores and vastly overestimates is seized with a nervous spasm of the oesophagus and has to restrict himself to two cups of milk a day, each of which takes him three hours to consume. All visits to the adored are effectively stopped, and he has no choice but to devote himself to the nourishment of his body. Or a man who can no longer carry the weight of the huge business he has built up is afflicted with nervous attacks of thirst and speedily falls a victim to hysterical alcoholism.

Hysteria is, in my view, by far the most frequent neurosis of the extraverted type. The hallmark of classic hysteria is an exaggerated rapport with persons in the immediate environment and an adjustment to surrounding conditions that amounts to imitation. A constant tendency to make himself interesting and to produce an impression is a basic feature of the hysteric. The corollary of this is his proverbial suggestibility, his proneness to another person's influence. Another unmistakable sign of the extraverted hysteric is his effusiveness, which occasionally carries him into the realm of fantasy, so that he is accused of the "hysterical lie." The hysterical character begins as an exaggeration of the normal attitude; it is then complicated by compensatory reactions from the uncon-

---

[2][For a detailed discussion of this case see *Analytical Psychology: Its Theory and Practice*, pp. 87ff.—EDITORS.]

scious, which counteract the exaggerated extraversion by means of physical symptoms that force the libido to introvert. The reaction of the unconscious produces another class of symptoms having a more introverted character, one of the most typical being a morbid intensification of fantasy activity.

After this general outline of the extraverted attitude we shall now turn to a description of the modifications which the basic psychological functions undergo as a result of this attitude.

b. The Attitude of the Unconscious

It may perhaps seem odd that I should speak of an "attitude of the unconscious." As I have repeatedly indicated, I regard the attitude of the unconscious as compensatory to consciousness. According to this view, the unconscious has as good a claim to an "attitude" as the latter.

In the preceding section I emphasized the tendency to one-sidedness in the extraverted attitude, due to the ascendency of the object over the course of psychic events. The extraverted type is constantly tempted to expend himself for the apparent benefit of the object, to assimilate subject to object. I have discussed in some detail the harmful consequences of an exaggeration of the extraverted attitude, namely, the suppression of the subjective factor. It is only to be expected, therefore, that the psychic compensation of the conscious extraverted attitude will lay special weight on the subjective factor, and that we shall find a markedly egocentric tendency in the unconscious. Practical experience proves this to be the case. I do not wish to cite case material at this point, so must refer my readers to the ensuing sections, where I try to present the characteristic attitude of the unconscious in each function-type. In this section we are concerned simply with the compensation of the extraverted attitude in general, so I shall confine myself to describing the attitude of the unconscious in equally general terms.

The attitude of the unconscious as an effective complement to the conscious extraverted attitude has a definitely introverting character. It concentrates the libido on the subjective factor, that is, on all those needs and demands that are stifled or repressed by the conscious attitude. As may be gathered from what was said in the previous section, a purely objective orientation does violence to a multitude of subjective impulses, intentions, needs, and desires and deprives them of the libido that is their natural right. Man is not a machine that can be remodelled for quite other purposes as occasion demands, in the hope that it will go on functioning as regularly as before but in a quite different way. He carries his whole history with him; in his very structure is written the history of mankind. This historical element in man represents a vital need to which a wise psychic economy must respond. Somehow the past must come alive and participate in the present. Total assimilation to the object will always arouse the protest of the suppressed minority of those elements that belong to the past and have existed from the very beginning.

From these general considerations it is easy to see why the unconscious demands of the extravert have an essentially primitive, infantile, egocentric character. When Freud says that the unconscious "can do nothing but wish" this is very largely true of the unconscious of the extravert. His adjustment to the objective situation and his assimilation to the object prevent low-powered subjective impulses from reaching consciousness. These impulses (thoughts, wishes, affects, needs, feelings, etc.) take on a regressive character according to the degree of repression; the less they are acknowledged, the more infantile and archaic they become. The conscious attitude robs them of all energy that is readily disposable, only leaving them the energy of which it cannot deprive them. This residue, which still possesses a potency not to be underestimated, can be described only as primordial instinct. Instinct can never be eradicated in an individual by arbitrary measures; it requires the slow, organic transformation of many generations to effect a radical change, for instinct is the energic expression of the organism's make-up.

Thus with every repressed impulse a considerable amount of energy ultimately remains, of an instinctive character, and preserves its potency despite the deprivation that made it unconscious. The more complete the conscious attitude of extraversion is, the more infantile and archaic the unconscious attitude will be. The egoism which characterizes the extravert's unconscious attitude goes far beyond mere childish selfishness; it verges on the ruthless and the brutal. Here we find in full flower the incest-wish described by Freud. It goes without saying that these things are entirely unconscious and remain hidden from the layman so long as the extraversion of the conscious attitude is not extreme. But whenever it is exaggerated, the unconscious comes to light in symptomatic form; its egoism, infantilism, and archaism lose their original compensatory character and appear in more or less open opposition to the conscious attitude. This begins as an absurd exaggeration of conscious standpoint, aiming at a further repression of the unconscious, but usually it ends in a *reductio ad absurdum* of the conscious attitude and hence in catastrophe. The catastrophe may take an objective form, since the objective aims gradually become falsified by the subjective. I remember the case of a printer who, starting as a mere employee, worked his way up after years of hard struggle till at last he became the owner of a flourishing business. The more it expanded, the more it tightened its hold on him, until finally it swallowed up all his other interests. This proved his ruin. As an unconscious compensation of his exclusive interest in the business, certain memories of his childhood came to life. As a child he had taken great delight in painting and drawing. But instead of renewing this capacity for its own sake as a compensating hobby, he channelled it into his business and began wondering how he might embellish his products in an "artistic" way. Unfortunately his fantasies materialized: he actually turned out stuff that suited his own primitive and infantile taste, with the result that after a very few years his business went to pieces. He acted in accordance with one of our "cultural ideals," which says that any enterprising person has to concentrate everything on the one aim in view. But he went too far, and merely fell a victim to the power of his infantile demands.

The catastrophe can, however, also be subjective and take the form of a nervous breakdown. This invariably happens when the influence of the unconscious finally paralyzes all conscious action. The demands of the unconscious then force themselves imperiously on consciousness and bring about a disastrous split which shows itself in one of two ways: either the subject no longer knows what he really wants and nothing interests him, or he wants too much at once and has too many interests, but in impossible things. The suppression of infantile and primitive demands for cultural reasons easily leads to a neurosis or to the abuse of narcotics such as alcohol, morphine, cocaine, etc. In more extreme cases the split ends in suicide.

It is an outstanding peculiarity of unconscious impulses that, when deprived of energy by lack of conscious recognition, they take on a destructive character, and this happens as soon as they cease to be compensatory. Their compensatory function ceases as soon as they reach a depth corresponding to a cultural level absolutely incompatible with our own. From this moment the unconscious impulses form a block in every way opposed to the conscious attitude, and its very existence leads to open conflict.

Generally speaking, the compensating attitude of the unconscious finds expression in the maintenance of the psychic equilibrium. A normal extraverted attitude does not, of course, mean that the individual invariably behaves in accordance with the extraverted schema. Even in the same individual many psychological processes may be observed that involve the mechanism of introversion. We call a mode of behaviour extraverted only when the mechanism of extraversion predominates. In these cases the most differentiated function is always employed in an extraverted way, whereas the inferior functions are introverted; in other words, the superior function is the most conscious one and completely under conscious control, whereas the less differentiated functions are in part unconscious and far less under the control of consciousness. The superior function is always an expression of the conscious personality, of its aims, will, and general performance, whereas the less differentiated functions fall into the category of things that simply "happen" to one. These things need not be mere slips of the tongue or pen and other such oversights, they can equally well be half or three-quarters intended, for the less differentiated functions also possess a slight degree of consciousness. A classic example of this is the extraverted feeling type, who enjoys an excellent feeling rapport with the people around him, yet occasionally "happens" to express opinions of unsurpassable tactlessness. These opinions spring from his inferior and half-conscious thinking, which, being only partly under his control and insufficiently related to the object, can be quite ruthless in its effects.

The less differentiated functions of the extravert always show a highly subjective colouring with pronounced egocentricity and personal bias, thus revealing their close connection with the unconscious. The unconscious is continually coming to light through them. It should not be imagined that the unconscious lies permanently buried under so many overlying strata that it can only be uncovered, so to speak, by a laborious process of excavation. On the contrary, there is a constant influx of unconscious contents into the conscious psychological process, to such a degree that at times it is hard for the observer to decide which character traits belong to the conscious and which to the unconscious personality. This difficulty is met with mainly in people who are given to express themselves more profusely than others. Naturally it also depends very largely on the attitude of the observer whether he seizes hold of the conscious or the unconscious character of the personality. Generally speaking, a judging observer will tend to seize on the conscious character, while a perceptive observer will be more influenced by the unconscious character, since judgment is chiefly concerned with the conscious motivation of the psychic process, while perception registers the process itself. But in so far as we apply judgment and perception in equal measure, it may easily happen that a personality appears to us as both introverted and extraverted, so that we cannot decide at first to which attitude the superior function belongs. In such cases only a thorough analysis of the qualities of each function can help us to form a valid judgment. We must observe which function is completely under conscious control, and which functions have a haphazard and spontaneous character. The former is always more highly differentiated than the latter, which also possess infantile and primitive traits. Occasionally the superior function gives the impression of normality, while the others have something abnormal or pathological about them.

12

c. The Peculiarities of the Basic Psychological Functions in the Extraverted Attitude

Thinking

As a consequence of the general attitude of extraversion, thinking is oriented by the object and objective data. This gives rise to a noticeable peculiarity. Thinking in general is fed on the one hand from subjective and in the last resort unconscious sources, and on the other hand from objective data transmitted by sense-perception. Extraverted thinking is conditioned in a larger measure by the latter than by the former. Judgment always presupposes a criterion; for the extraverted judgment, the criterion supplied by external conditions is the valid and determining one, no matter whether it be represented directly by an objective, perceptible fact or by an objective idea; for an objective idea is equally determined by external data or borrowed from outside even when it is subjectively sanctioned. Extraverted thinking, therefore, need not necessarily be purely concretistic thinking; it can just as well be purely ideal thinking, if for instance it can be shown that the ideas it operates with are largely borrowed from outside, i.e., have been transmitted by tradition and education. So in judging whether a particular thinking is extraverted or not we must first ask: by what criterion does it judge—does it come from outside, or is its origin subjective? A further criterion is the direction the thinking takes in drawing conclusions—whether it is principally directed outwards or not. It is no proof of its extraverted nature that it is preoccupied with concrete objects, since my thinking may be preoccupied with a concrete object either because I am abstracting my thought from it or because I am concretizing my thought through it. Even when my thinking is preoccupied with concrete things and could be described as extraverted to that extent, the direction it will take still remains an essential characteristic and an open question—namely, whether or not in its further course it leads back again to objective data, external facts, or generally accepted ideas. So far as the practical thinking of the business man, the technician, or the scientific investigator is concerned, its outer-directedness is obvious enough. But in the

13

case of the philosopher it remains open to doubt when his thinking is directed to ideas. We then have to inquire whether these ideas are simply abstractions from objective experience, in which case they would represent higher collective concepts comprising a sum of objective facts, or whether (if they are clearly not abstractions from immediate experience) they may not be derived from tradition or borrowed from the intellectual atmosphere of the time. In the latter case, they fall into the category of objective data, and accordingly this thinking should be called extraverted.

Although I do not propose to discuss the nature of introverted thinking at this point, reserving it for a later section (pars. 628–31), it is essential that I should say a few words about it before proceeding further. For if one reflects on what I have just said about extraverted thinking, one might easily conclude that this covers everything that is ordinarily understood as thinking. A thinking that is directed neither to objective facts nor to general ideas, one might argue, scarcely deserves the name "thinking" at all. I am fully aware that our age and its most eminent representatives know and acknowledge only the extraverted type of thinking. This is largely because all the thinking that appears visibly on the surface in the form of science or philosophy or even art either derives directly from objects or else flows into general ideas. For both these reasons it appears essentially understandable, even though it may not always be self-evident, and it is therefore regarded as valid. In this sense it might be said that the extraverted intellect oriented by objective data is actually the only one that is recognized. But—and now I come to the question of the introverted intellect—there also exists an entirely different kind of thinking, to which the term "thinking" can hardly be denied: it is a kind that is oriented neither by immediate experience of objects nor by traditional ideas. I reach this other kind of thinking in the following manner: when my thoughts are preoccupied with a concrete object or a general idea, in such a way that the course of my thinking eventually leads me back to my starting-point, this intellectual process is not the only psychic process that is going on in me. I will disregard all those sensations and feelings which become noticeable as a more or less disturbing accompaniment to my train of thought, and will merely point out that this very thinking process which starts from the object and returns to the object also stands in a constant relation to the subject. This relation is a *sine qua non*, without which no thinking process whatsoever could take place. Even though my thinking process is directed, as far as possible, to objective data, it is still *my* subjective process, and it can neither avoid nor dispense with this admixture of subjectivity. Struggle as I may to give an objective orientation to my train of thought, I cannot shut out the parallel subjective process and its running accompaniment without extinguishing the very spark of life from my thought. This parallel process has a natural and hardly avoidable tendency to subjectify the objective data and assimilate them to the subject.

Now when the main accent lies on the subjective process, that other kind of thinking arises which is opposed to extraverted thinking, namely, that purely subjective orientation which I call introverted. This thinking is neither determined by objective data nor directed to them; it is a thinking that starts from the subject and is directed to subjective ideas or subjective facts. I do not wish to enter more fully into this kind of thinking here; I have merely established its existence as the necessary complement of extraverted thinking and brought it into clearer focus.

Extraverted thinking, then, comes into existence only when the objective orientation predominates. This fact does nothing to alter the logic of thinking; it merely constitutes that difference between thinkers which James considered a matter of temperament. Orientation to the object, as already explained, makes no essential change in the thinking function; only its appearance is altered. It has the appearance of being captivated by the object, as though without the external orientation it simply could not exist. It almost seems as though it were a mere sequela of external facts, or as though it could reach its highest point only when flowing into some general idea. It seems to be constantly affected by the objective data and to draw conclusions only with their consent. Hence it gives one the impression of a certain lack of freedom, of occasional short-sightedness, in spite of all its adroitness within the area circumscribed by the object. What I am describing is simply the impression this sort of thinking makes on the observer, who must himself have a different standpoint, otherwise it would be impossible for him to observe the phenomenon of extraverted thinking at all. But because of his different standpoint he sees only its outward aspect, not its essence, whereas the thinker himself can apprehend its essence but not its outward aspect. Judging by appearances can never do justice to the essence of the thing, hence the verdict is in most cases depreciatory.

In its essence this thinking is no less fruitful and creative than introverted thinking, it merely serves other ends. This difference becomes quite palpable when extraverted thinking appropriates material that is the special province of introverted thinking; when, for instance, a subjective conviction is explained analytically in terms of objective data or as being derived from objective ideas. For our scientific consciousness, however, the difference becomes even more obvious when introverted thinking attempts to bring objective data into connections not warranted by the object—in other words, to subordinate them to a subjective idea. Each type of thinking senses the other as an encroachment on its own province, and hence a sort of shadow effect is produced, each revealing to the other its least favourable aspect. Introverted thinking then appears as something quite arbitrary, while extraverted thinking seems dull and banal. Thus the two orientations are incessantly at war.

One might think it easy enough to put an end to this conflict by making a clear distinction between objective and subjective data. Unfortunately, this is impossible, though not a few have attempted it. And even if it were possible it would be a disastrous proceeding, since in themselves both orientations are one-sided and of limited validity, so that each needs the influence of the other. When objective data predominate over thinking to any great extent, thinking is sterilized, becoming a mere appendage of the object and no longer capable of abstracting itself into an independent concept. It is then reduced to a kind of "after-thought," by which I do not mean "reflection" but a purely imitative thinking which affirms nothing beyond what was visibly and immediately present in the objective data in the first place. This thinking naturally leads directly back to the object, but never beyond it, not even to a

linking of experience with an objective idea. Conversely, when it has an idea for an object, it is quite unable to experience its practical, individual value, but remains stuck in a more or less tautological position. The materialistic mentality is an instructive example of this.

When extraverted thinking is subordinated to objective data as a result of over-determination by the object, it engrosses itself entirely in the individual experience and accumulates a mass of undigested empirical material. The oppressive weight of individual experiences having little or no connection with one another produces a dissociation of thought which usually requires psychological compensation. This must consist in some simple, general idea that gives coherence to the disordered whole, or at least affords the possibility of such. Ideas like "matter" or "energy" serve this purpose. But when the thinking depends primarily not on objective data but on some second-hand idea, the very poverty of this thinking is compensated by an all the more impressive accumulation of facts congregating round a narrow and sterile point of view, with the result that many valuable and meaningful aspects are completely lost sight of. Many of the allegedly scientific outpourings of our own day owe their existence to this wrong orientation.

The Extraverted Thinking Type

It is a fact of experience that the basic psychological functions seldom or never all have the same strength or degree of development in the same individual. As a rule, one or the other function predominates, in both strength and development. When thinking holds prior place among the psychological functions, i.e., when the life of an individual is mainly governed by reflective thinking so that every important action proceeds, or is intended to proceed, from intellectually considered motives, we may fairly call this a thinking type. Such a type may be either introverted or extraverted. We will first discuss the extraverted thinking type.

This type will, by definition, be a man whose constant endeavour—in so far, of course, as he is a pure type—is to make all his activities dependent on intellectual conclusions, which in the last resort are always oriented by objective data, whether these be external facts or generally accepted ideas. This type of man elevates objective reality, or an objectively oriented intellectual formula, into the ruling principle not only for himself but for his whole environment. By this formula good and evil are measured, and beauty and ugliness determined. Everything that agrees with this formula is right, everything that contradicts it is wrong, and anything that passes by it indifferently is merely incidental. Because this formula seems to embody the entire meaning of life, it is made into a universal law which must be put into effect everywhere all the time, both individually and collectively. Just as the extraverted thinking type subordinates himself to his formula, so, for their own good, everybody round him must obey it too, for whoever refuses to obey it is wrong—he is resisting the universal law, and is therefore unreasonable, immoral, and without a conscience. His moral code forbids him to tolerate exceptions; his ideal must under all circumstances be realized, for in his eyes it is the purest conceivable formulation of objective reality, and therefore must also be a universally valid truth, quite indispensable for the salvation of mankind. This is not from any great love for his neighbour, but from the higher standpoint of justice and truth. Anything in his own nature that appears to invalidate this formula is a mere imperfection, an accidental failure, something to be eliminated on the next occasion, or, in the event of further failure, clearly pathological. If tolerance for the sick, the suffering, or the abnormal should chance to be an ingredient of the formula, special provisions will be made for humane societies, hospitals, prisons, missions, etc., or at least extensive plans will be drawn up. Generally the motive of justice and truth is not sufficient to ensure the actual execution of such projects; for this, real Christian charity is needed, and this has more to do with feeling than with any intellectual formula. "Oughts" and "musts" bulk large in this programme. If the formula is broad enough, this type may play a very useful role in social life as a reformer or public prosecutor or purifier of conscience, or as the propagator of important innovations. But the more rigid the formula, the more he develops into a martinet, a quibbler, and a prig, who would like to force himself and others into one mould. Here we have the two extremes between which the majority of these types move.

In accordance with the nature of the extraverted attitude, the influence and activities of these personalities are the more favourable and beneficial the further from the centre their radius extends. Their best aspect is to be found at the periphery of their sphere of influence. The deeper we penetrate into their own power province, the more we feel the unfavourable effects of their tyranny. A quite different life pulses at the periphery, where the truth of the formula can be felt as a valuable adjunct to the rest. But the closer we come to centre of power where the formula operates, the more life withers away from everything that does not conform to its dictates. Usually it is the nearest relatives who have to taste the unpleasant consequences of the extraverted formula, since they are the first to receive its relentless benefits. But in the end it is the subject himself who suffers most—and this brings us to the reverse side of the psychology of this type.

The fact that an intellectual formula never has been and never will be devised which could embrace and express the manifold possibilities of life must lead to the inhibition or exclusion of other activities and ways of living that are just as important. In the first place, all those activities that are dependent on feeling will become repressed in such a type—for instance, aesthetic activities, taste, artistic sense, cultivation of friends, etc. Irrational phenomena such as religious experiences, passions, and suchlike are often repressed to the point of complete unconsciousness. Doubtless there are exceptional people who are able to sacrifice their entire life to a particular formula, but for most of us such exclusiveness is impossible in the long run. Sooner or later, depending on outer circumstances or inner disposition, the potentialities repressed by the intellectual attitude will make themselves indirectly felt by disturbing the conscious conduct of life. When the disturbance reaches a definite pitch, we speak of a neurosis. In most cases it does not go so far, because the individual instinctively allows himself extenuating modifications of his formula in a suitably rationalistic guise, thus creating a safety valve.

The relative or total unconsciousness of the tendencies and functions excluded by the conscious attitude keeps them in an undeveloped state. In comparison with the conscious function they are inferior. To the extent that they are unconscious, they become merged with the rest of the unconscious contents and acquire a bizarre character. To the extent that they are conscious, they play only a secondary role, though one of considerable importance for the over-all psychological picture. The first function to be affected by the conscious inhibition is feeling, since it is the most opposed to the rigid intellectual formula and is therefore repressed the most intensely. No function can be entirely eliminated—it can only be greatly distorted. In so far as feeling is compliant and lets itself be subordinated, it has to support the conscious attitude and adapt to its aims. But this is possible only up to a point; part of it remains refractory and has to be repressed. If the repression is successful, the subliminal feeling then functions in a way that is opposed to the conscious aims, even producing effects whose cause is a complete enigma to the individual. For example, the conscious altruism of this type, which is often quite extraordinary, may be thwarted by a secret self-seeking which gives a selfish twist to actions that in themselves are disinterested. Purely ethical intentions may lead him into critical situations which sometimes have more than a semblance of being the outcome of motives far from ethical. There are guardians of public morals who suddenly find themselves in compromising situations, or rescue workers who are themselves in dire need of rescue. Their desire to save others leads them to employ means which are calculated to bring about the very thing they wished to avoid. There are extraverted idealists so consumed by their desire for the salvation of mankind that they will not shrink from any lie or trickery in pursuit of their ideal. In science there are not a few painful examples of highly respected investigators who are so convinced of the truth and general validity of their formula that they have not scrupled to falsify evidence in its favour. Their sanction is: the end justifies the means. Only an inferior feeling function, operating unconsciously and in secret, could seduce otherwise reputable men into such aberrations.

The inferiority of feeling in this type also manifests itself in other ways. In keeping with the objective formula, the conscious attitude becomes more or less impersonal, often to such a degree that personal interests suffer. If the attitude is extreme, all personal considerations are lost sight of, even those affecting the subject's own person. His health is neglected, his social position deteriorates, the most vital interests of his family—health, finances, morals—are violated for the sake of the ideal. Personal sympathy with others must in any case suffer unless they too happen to espouse the same ideal. Often the closest members of his family, his own children, know such a father only as a cruel tyrant, while the outside world resounds with the fame of his humanity. Because of the highly impersonal character of the conscious attitude, the unconscious feelings are extremely personal and oversensitive, giving rise to secret prejudices—a readiness, for instance, to misconstrue any opposition to his formula as personal ill-will, or a constant tendency to make negative assumptions about other people in order to invalidate their arguments in advance—in defence, naturally, of his own touchiness. His unconscious sensitivity makes him sharp in tone, acrimonious, aggressive. Insinuations multiply. His feelings have a sultry and resentful character— always a mark of the inferior function. Magnanimous as he may be in sacrificing himself to his intellectual goal, his feelings are petty, mistrustful, crotchety, and conservative. Anything new that is not already contained in his formula is seen through a veil of unconscious hatred and condemned accordingly. As late as the middle of the last century a certain doctor, famed for his humanitarianism, threatened to dismiss an assistant for daring to use a thermometer, because the formula decreed that temperature must be taken by the pulse.

The more the feelings are repressed, the more deleterious is their secret influence on thinking that is otherwise beyond reproach. The intellectual formula, which because of its intrinsic value might justifiably claim general recognition, undergoes a characteristic alteration as a result of this unconscious personal sensitiveness: it becomes rigidly dogmatic. The self-assertion of the personality is transferred to the formula. Truth is no longer allowed to speak for itself; it is identified with the subject and treated like a sensitive darling whom an evil-minded critic has wronged. The critic is demolished, if possible with personal invective, and no argument is too gross to be used against him. The truth must be trotted out, until finally it begins to dawn on the public that it is not so much a question of truth as of its personal begetter.

The dogmatism of the intellectual formula sometimes undergoes further characteristic alterations, due not so much to the unconscious admixture of repressed personal feelings as to a contamination with other unconscious factors which have become fused with them. Although reason itself tells us that every intellectual formula can never be anything more than a partial truth and can never claim general validity, in practice the formula gains such an ascendency that all other possible standpoints are thrust into the background. It usurps the place of all more general, less definite, more modest and therefore more truthful views of life. It even supplants that general view of life we call religion. Thus the formula becomes a religion, although in essentials it has not the slightest connection with anything religious. At the same time, it assumes the essentially religious quality of absoluteness. It becomes an intellectual superstition. But now all the psychological tendencies it has repressed build up a counter-position in the unconscious and give rise to paroxysms of doubt. The more it tries to fend off the doubt, the more fanatical the conscious attitude becomes, for fanaticism is nothing but over-compensated doubt. This development ultimately leads to an exaggerated defence of the conscious position and to the formation of a counter-position in the unconscious absolutely opposed to it; for instance, conscious rationalism is opposed by an extreme irrationality, and a scientific attitude by one that is archaic and superstitious. This explains those bigoted and ridiculous views well-known in the history of science which have proved stumbling-blocks to many an eminent investigator. Frequently the unconscious counter-position is embodied in a woman. In my experience this type is found chiefly among men, since, in general, thinking tends more often to be a dominant function in men than in women. When thinking dominates in a woman it is usually associated with a predominantly *intuitive* cast of mind.

The thinking of the extraverted type is *positive*, i.e., productive. It leads to the discovery of new facts or to general conceptions based on disparate empirical material. It is usually synthetic too. Even when it analyses it constructs, because it is always advancing beyond the analysis to a new combination, to a further conception which reunites the analysed material in a different way or adds something to it. One could call this kind of judgment *predicative*. A characteristic feature, at any rate, is that it is never absolutely depreciative or destructive, since it always substitutes a fresh value for the one destroyed. This is because the thinking of this type is the main channel into which his vital energy flows. The steady flow of life manifests itself in his thinking, so that his thought has a progressive, creative quality. It is not stagnant or regressive. But it can become so if it fails to retain prior place in his consciousness. In that case it loses the quality of a positive, vital activity. It follows in the wake of other functions and becomes Epimethean, plagued by afterthoughts, contenting itself with constant broodings on things past and gone, chewing them over in an effort to analyse and digest them. Since the creative element is now lodged in another function, thinking no longer progresses: it stagnates. Judgment takes on a distinct quality of *inherence*: it confines itself entirely to the range of the given material, nowhere overstepping it. It is satisfied with more or less abstract statements which do not impart any value to the material that is not already inherent in it. Such judgments are always oriented to the object, and they affirm nothing more about an experience than its objective and intrinsic meaning. We may easily observe this type of thinking in people who cannot refrain from tacking on to an impression or experience some rational and doubtless very valid remark which in no way ventures beyond the charmed circle of the objective datum. At bottom such a remark merely says: "I have understood it because afterwards I can think it." And there the matter ends. At best such a judgment amounts to no more than putting the experience in an objective setting, where it quite obviously belonged in the first place.

But whenever a function other than thinking predominates in consciousness to any marked degree, thinking, so far as it is conscious at all and not directly dependent on the dominant function, assumes a negative character. If it is subordinated to the dominant function it may actually wear a positive aspect, but closer scrutiny will show that it simply mimics the dominant function, supporting it with arguments that clearly contradict the laws of logic proper to thinking. This kind of thinking is of no interest for our present discussion. Our concern is rather with the nature of a thinking which cannot subordinate itself to another function but remains true to its own principle. To observe and investigate this thinking is not easy, because it is more or less constantly repressed by the conscious attitude. Hence, in the majority of cases, it must first be retrieved from the background of consciousness, unless it should come to the surface accidentally in some unguarded moment. As a rule it has to be enticed with some such question as "Now what do you *really* think?" or "What is your private view of the matter?" Or perhaps one may have to use a little cunning, framing the question something like this: "What do you imagine, then, that *I* really think about it?" One should adopt this device when the real thinking is unconscious and therefore projected. The thinking that is enticed to the surface in this way has characteristic qualities, and it was these I had in mind when I described it as negative. Its habitual mode is best expressed by the two words "nothing but." Goethe personified this thinking in the figure of Mephistopheles. Above all it shows a distinct tendency to trace the object of its judgment back to some banality or other, thus stripping it of any significance in its own right. The trick is to make it appear dependent on something quite commonplace. Whenever a conflict arises between two men over something apparently objective and impersonal, negative thinking mutters "Cherchez la femme." Whenever somebody defends or advocates a cause, negative thinking never asks about its importance but simply: "What does *he* get out of it?" The dictum ascribed to Moleschott, "Der Mensch ist, was er isst" (man is what he eats, or, rendered more freely, what you eat you are), likewise comes under this heading, as do many other aphorisms I need not quote here.

The destructive quality of this thinking, as well as its limited usefulness on occasion, does not need stressing. But there is still another form of negative thinking, which at first glance might not be recognized as such, and that is *theosophical* thinking, which today is rapidly spreading in all parts of the world, presumably in reaction to the materialism of the recent past. Theosophical thinking has an air that is not in the least reductive, since it exalts everything to a transcendental and world-embracing idea. A dream, for instance, is no longer just a dream, but an experience "on another plane." The hitherto inexplicable fact of telepathy is very simply explained as "vibrations" passing from one person to another. An ordinary nervous complaint is explained by the fact that something has collided with the "astral body." Certain ethnological peculiarities of the dwellers on the Atlantic seaboard are easily accounted for by the submergence of Atlantis, and so on. We have only to open a theosophical book to be overwhelmed by the realization that everything is already explained, and that "spiritual science" has left no enigmas unsolved. But, at bottom, this kind of thinking is just as negative as materialistic thinking. When the latter regards psychology as chemical changes in the ganglia or as the extrusion and retraction of cell-pseudopodia or as an internal secretion, this is just as much a superstition as theosophy. The only difference is that materialism reduces everything to physiology, whereas theosophy reduces everything to Indian metaphysics. When a dream is traced back to an overloaded stomach, this is no explanation of the dream, and when we explain telepathy as vibrations we have said just as little. For what are "vibrations"? Not only are both methods of explanation futile, they are actually destructive, because by diverting interest away from the main issue, in one case to the stomach and in the other to imaginary vibrations, they hamper any serious investigation of the problem by a bogus explanation. Either kind of thinking is sterile and sterilizing. Its negative quality is due to the fact that it is so indescribably cheap, impoverished, and lacking in creative energy. It is a thinking taken in tow by other functions.

Feeling

Feeling in the extraverted attitude is likewise oriented by objective data, the object being the indispensable determinant of the quality of feeling. The extravert's feeling is always in harmony with objective values. For anyone who has known feeling only as something subjective, the nature of extraverted feeling will be difficult to grasp, because it has detached itself as much as possible from the subjective factor and subordinated itself entirely to the influence of the object. Even when it appears not to be qualified by a concrete object, it is none the less still under the spell of traditional or generally accepted values of some kind. I may feel moved, for instance, to say that something is "beautiful" or "good," not because I find it "beautiful" or "good" from my own subjective feeling about it, but because it is fitting and politic to call it so, since a contrary judgment would upset the general feeling situation. A feeling judgment of this kind is not by any means a pretence or a lie, it is simply an act of adjustment. A painting, for instance, is called "beautiful" because a painting hung in a drawing room and bearing a well-known signature is generally assumed to be beautiful, or because to call it "hideous" would presumably offend the family of its fortunate possessor, or because the visitor wants to create a pleasant feeling atmosphere, for which purpose everything must be felt as agreeable. These feelings are governed by an objective criterion. As such they are genuine, and represent the feeling function as a whole.

In precisely the same way as extraverted thinking strives to rid itself of subjective influences, extraverted feeling has to undergo a process of differentiation before it is finally denuded of every subjective trimming. The valuations resulting from the act of feeling either correspond directly with objective values or accord with traditional and generally accepted standards. This kind of feeling is very largely responsible for the fact that so many people flock to the theatre or to concerts, or go to church, and do so moreover with their feelings correctly adjusted. Fashions, too, owe their whole existence to it, and, what is far more valuable, the positive support of social, philanthropic, and other such cultural institutions. In these matters extraverted feeling proves itself a creative factor. Without it, a harmonious social life would be impossible. To that extent extraverted feeling is just as beneficial and sweetly reasonable in its effects as extraverted thinking. But these salutary effects are lost as soon as the object gains ascendency. The force of extraverted feeling then pulls the personality into the object, the object assimilates him, whereupon the personal quality of the feeling, which constitutes its chief charm, disappears. It becomes cold, "unfeeling," untrustworthy. It has ulterior motives, or at least makes an impartial observer suspect them. It no longer makes that agreeable and refreshing impression which invariably accompanies genuine feeling; instead, one suspects a pose, or that the person is acting, even though he

26

may be quite unconscious of any egocentric motives. Over-extraverted feeling may satisfy aesthetic expectations, but it does not speak to the heart; it appeals merely to the senses or —worse still—only to reason. It can provide the aesthetic padding for a situation, but there it stops, and beyond that its effect is nil. It has become sterile. If this process goes any further, a curiously contradictory dissociation of feeling results: everything becomes an object of feeling valuations, and innumerable relationships are entered into which are all at variance with each other. As this situation would become quite impossible if the subject received anything like due emphasis, even the last vestiges of a real personal standpoint are suppressed. The subject becomes so enmeshed in the network of individual feeling processes that to the observer it seems as though there were merely a feeling process and no longer a subject of feeling. Feeling in this state has lost all human warmth; it gives the impression of being put on, fickle, unreliable, and in the worst cases hysterical.

The Extraverted Feeling Type

As feeling is undeniably a more obvious characteristic of feminine psychology than thinking, the most pronounced feeling types are to be found among women. When extraverted feeling predominates we speak of an extraverted feeling type. Examples of this type that I can call to mind are, almost without exception, women. The woman of this type follows her feeling as a guide throughout life. As a result of upbringing her feeling has developed into an adjusted function subject to conscious control. Except in extreme cases, her feeling has a personal quality, even though she may have repressed the subjective factor to a large extent. Her personality appears adjusted in relation to external conditions. Her feelings harmonize with objective situations and general values. This is seen nowhere more clearly than in her love choice: the "suitable" man is loved, and no one else; he is suitable not because he appeals to her hidden subjective nature—about which she usually knows nothing—but because he comes up to all reasonable expectations in the matter of age, position, income, size and respectability of his family, etc. One could easily reject such a picture as ironical or cynical, but I am fully convinced that the love feeling of this type of woman is in perfect accord with her choice. It is genuine and not just shrewd. There are countless "reasonable" marriages of this kind and they are by no means the worst. These women are good companions and excellent mothers so long as the husbands and children are blessed with the conventional psychic constitution.

But one can feel "correctly" only when feeling is not disturbed by anything else. Nothing disturbs feeling so much as thinking. It is therefore understandable that in this type thinking will be kept in abeyance as much as possible. This does not mean that the woman does not think at all; on the contrary, she may think a great deal and very cleverly, but her thinking is never *sui generis*—it is an Epimethean appendage to her feeling. What she cannot feel, she cannot consciously think. "But I can't think what I don't feel," such a type said to me once in indignant tones. So far as her feeling allows, she can think very well, but every conclusion, however logical, that might lead to a disturbance of feeling is rejected at the outset. It is simply not thought. Thus everything that fits in with objective values is good, and is loved, and everything else seems to her to exist in a world apart.

But a change comes over the picture when the importance of the object reaches a still higher level. As already explained, the subject then becomes so assimilated to the object that the subject of feeling is completely engulfed. Feeling loses its personal quality, and becomes feeling for its own sake; the personality seems wholly dissolved in the feeling of the moment. But since actual life is a constant succession of situations that evoke different and even contradictory feelings, the personality gets split up into as many different feeling states. At one moment one is this, at another something quite different—to all appearances, for in reality such a multiple personality is impossible. The basis of the ego always remains the same and consequently finds itself at odds with the changing feeling states. To the observer, therefore, the display of feeling no longer appears as a personal expression of the subject but as an alteration of the ego—a mood, in other words. Depending on the degree of dissociation between the ego and the momentary state of feeling, signs of self-disunity will become clearly apparent, because the originally compensatory attitude of the unconscious has turned into open opposition. This shows itself first of all in extravagant displays of feeling, gushing talk, loud expostulations, etc., which ring hollow: "The lady doth protest too much." It is at once apparent that some kind of resistance is being over-compensated, and one begins to wonder whether these demonstrations might not turn out quite different. And a little later they do. Only a very slight alteration in the situation is needed to call forth at once just the opposite pronouncement on the selfsame object. As a result of these experiences the observer is unable to take either pronouncement seriously. He begins to reserve judgment. But since, for this type, it is of the highest importance to establish an intense feeling of rapport with the environment, redoubled efforts are now required to overcome this reserve. Thus, in the manner of a vicious circle, the situation goes from bad to worse. The stronger the feeling relation to the object, the more the unconscious opposition comes to the surface.

We have already seen that the extraverted feeling type suppresses thinking most of all because this is the function most liable to disturb feeling. For the same reason, thinking totally shuts out feeling if ever it wants to reach any kind of pure results, for nothing is more liable to prejudice and falsify thinking than feeling values. But, as I have said, though the thinking of the extraverted feeling type is repressed as an independent function, the repression is not complete; it is repressed only so far as its inexorable logic drives it to conclusions that are incompatible with feeling. It is suffered to exist as a servant of feeling, or rather as its slave. Its backbone is broken; it may not operate on its own account, in accordance with its own laws. But since logic nevertheless exists and enforces its inexorable conclusions, this must take place somewhere, and it takes place outside consciousness, namely in the unconscious. Accordingly the unconscious of this type contains first and foremost a peculiar kind of thinking, a thinking that is infantile, archaic, negative. So long as the conscious feeling preserves its personal quality, or, to put it another way, so long as the personality is not swallowed up in successive states of feeling, this unconscious thinking remains compensatory. But as soon as the personality is dissociated and dissolves into a succession of contradictory feeling states, the identity of the ego is lost and the subject lapses into the unconscious. When this happens, it gets associated with the unconscious thinking processes and occasionally helps them to the surface. The stronger the conscious feeling is and the more ego-less it becomes, the stronger grows the unconscious opposition. The unconscious thoughts gravitate round just the most valued objects and mercilessly strip them of their value. The "nothing but" type of thinking comes into its own here, since it effectively depotentiates all feelings that are bound to the object. The unconscious thinking reaches the surface in the form of obsessive ideas which are invariably of a negative and depreciatory character. Women of this type have moments when the most hideous thoughts fasten on the very objects most valued by their feelings. This negative thinking utilizes every infantile prejudice or comparison for the deliberate purpose of casting aspersions on the feeling value, and musters every primitive instinct in the attempt to come out with "nothing but" interpretations. It need hardly be remarked that this procedure also mobilizes the collective unconscious and activates its store of primordial images, thus bringing with it the possibility of a regeneration of attitude on a different basis. Hysteria, with the characteristic infantile sexuality of its unconscious world of ideas, is the principal form of neurosis in this type.

Summary of the Extraverted Rational Types

I call the two preceding types rational or judging types because they are characterized by the supremacy of the reasoning and judging functions. It is a general distinguishing mark of both types that their life is, to a great extent, subordinated to rational judgment. But we have to consider whether by "rational" we are speaking from the standpoint of the individual's subjective psychology or from that of the observer, who perceives and judges from without. This observer could easily arrive at a contrary judgment, especially if he intuitively apprehended merely the outward behaviour of the person observed and judged accordingly. On the whole, the life of this type is never dependent on rational judgment alone; it is influenced in almost equal degree by unconscious irrationality. If observation is restricted to outward behaviour, without any concern for the internal economy of the individual's consciousness, one may get an even stronger impression of the irrational and fortuitous nature of certain unconscious manifestations than of the reasonableness of his conscious intentions and motivations. I therefore base my judgment on what the individual feels to be his conscious psychology. But I am willing to grant that one could equally well conceive and present such a psychology from precisely the opposite angle. I am also convinced that, had I myself chanced to possess a different psychology, I would have described the rational types in the reverse way, from the standpoint of the unconscious—as irrational, therefore. This aggravates the difficulty of a lucid presentation of psychological matters and immeasurably increases the possibility of misunderstandings. The arguments provoked by these misunderstandings are, as a rule, quite hopeless because each side is speaking at cross purposes. This experience is one reason the more for basing my presentation on the conscious psychology of the individual, since there at least we have a definite objective footing, which completely drops away the moment we try to base our psychological rationale on the unconscious. For in that case the observed object would have no voice in the matter at all, because there is nothing about which he is more uninformed than his own unconscious. The judgment is then left entirely to the subjective observer—a sure guarantee that it will be based on his own individual psychology, which would be forcibly imposed on the observed. To my mind, this is the case with the psychologies of both Freud and Adler. The individual is completely at the mercy of the judging observer, which can never be the case when the conscious psychology of the observed is accepted as a basis. He after all is the only competent judge, since he alone knows his conscious motives.

The rationality that characterizes the conscious conduct of life in both these types involves a deliberate exclusion of everything irrational and accidental. Rational judgment, in such a psychology, is a force that coerces the untidiness and fortuitousness of life into a definite pattern, or at least tries to do so. A definite choice is made from among all the possibilities it offers, only the rational ones being accepted; but on the other hand the independence and influence of the psychic functions which aid the perception of life's happenings are consequently restricted. Naturally this restriction of sensation and intuition is not absolute. These functions exist as before, but their products are subject to the choice made by rational judgment. It is not the intensity of a sensation as such that decides action, for instance, but judgment. Thus, in a sense, the functions of perception share the same fate as feeling in the case of the first type, or thinking in that of the second. They are relatively repressed, and therefore in an inferior state of differentiation. This gives a peculiar stamp to the unconscious of both our types: what they consciously and intentionally do accords with reason (*their* reason, of course), but what happens to them accords with the nature of infantile, primitive sensations and intuitions. At all events, what happens to these types is irrational (from their standpoint). But since there are vast numbers of people whose lives consist more of what happens to them than of actions governed by rational intentions, such a person, after observing them closely, might easily describe both our types as irrational. And one has to admit that only too often a man's unconscious makes a far stronger impression on an observer than his consciousness does, and that his actions are of considerably more importance than his rational intentions.

The rationality of both types is object-oriented and dependent on objective data. It accords with what is collectively considered to be rational. For them, nothing is rational save what is generally considered as such. Reason, however, is in large part subjective and individual. In our types this part is repressed, and increasingly so as the object gains in importance. Both the subject and his subjective reason, therefore, are in constant danger of repression, and when they succumb to it they fall under the tyranny of the unconscious, which in this case possesses very unpleasant qualities. Of its peculiar thinking we have already spoken. But, besides that, there are primitive sensations that express themselves compulsively, for instance in the form of compulsive pleasure-seeking in every conceivable form; there are also primitive intuitions that can become a positive torture to the person concerned and to everybody in his vicinity. Everything that is unpleasant and painful, everything that is disgusting, hateful, and evil, is sniffed out or suspected, and in most cases it is a half-truth calculated to provoke misunderstandings of the most poisonous kind. The antagonistic unconscious elements are so strong that they frequently disrupt the conscious rule of reason; the individual becomes the victim of chance happenings, which exercise a compulsive influence over him either because they pander to his sensations or because he intuits their unconscious significance.

Sensation

Sensation, in the extraverted attitude, is pre-eminently conditioned by the object. As sense perception, sensation is naturally dependent on objects. But, just as naturally, it is also dependent on the subject, for which reason there is subjective sensation of a kind entirely different from objective sensation. In the extraverted attitude the subjective component of sensation, so far as its conscious application is concerned, is either inhibited or repressed. Similarly, as an irrational function, sensation is largely repressed when thinking or feeling holds prior place; that is to say, it is a conscious function only to the extent that the rational attitude of consciousness permits accidental perceptions to become conscious contents—in a word, registers them. The sensory function is, of course, absolute in the stricter sense; everything is seen or heard, for instance, to the physiological limit, but not everything attains the threshold value a perception must have in order to be apperceived. It is different when sensation itself is paramount instead of merely seconding another function. In this case no element of objective sensation is excluded and nothing is repressed (except the subjective component already mentioned).

As sensation is chiefly conditioned by the object, those objects that excite the strongest sensations will be decisive for the individual's psychology. The result is a strong sensuous tie to the object. Sensation is therefore a vital function equipped with the strongest vital instinct. Objects are valued in so far as they excite sensations, and, so far as lies within the power of sensation, they are fully accepted into consciousness whether they are compatible with rational judgments or not. The sole criterion of their value is the intensity of the sensation produced by their objective qualities. Accordingly, all objective processes which excite any sensations at all make their appearance in consciousness. However, it is only concrete, sensuously perceived objects or processes that excite sensations for the extravert; those, exclusively, which everyone everywhere would sense as concrete. Hence the orientation of such an individual accords with purely sensuous reality. The judging, rational functions are subordinated to the concrete facts of sensation, and thus have all the qualities of the less differentiated functions, exhibiting negative, infantile, and archaic traits. The function most repressed is naturally the opposite of sensation —intuition, the function of unconscious perception.

The Extraverted Sensation Type

No other human type can equal the extraverted sensation type in realism. His sense for objective facts is extraordinarily developed. His life is an accumulation of actual experiences of concrete objects, and the more pronounced his type, the less use does he make of his experience. In certain cases the events in his life hardly deserve the name "experience" at all. What he experiences serves at most as a guide to fresh sensations; anything new that comes within his range of interest is acquired by way of sensation and has to serve its ends. Since one is inclined to regard a highly developed reality-sense as a sign of rationality, such people will be esteemed as very rational. But in actual fact this is not the case, since they are just as much at the mercy of their sensations in the face of irrational, chance happenings as they are in the face of rational ones. This type— the majority appear to be men—naturally does not think he is at the "mercy" of sensation. He would ridicule this view as quite beside the point, because sensation for him is a concrete expression of life—it is simply real life lived to the full. His whole aim is concrete enjoyment, and his morality is oriented accordingly. Indeed, true enjoyment has its own special morality, its own moderation and lawfulness, its own unselfishness and willingness to make sacrifices. It by no means follows that he is just sensual or gross, for he may differentiate his sensation to the finest pitch of aesthetic purity without ever deviating from his principle of concrete sensation however abstract his sensations may be. Wulfen's *Der Genussmensch: ein Cicerone im rücksichtslosen Lebensgenuss*[3] is the unvarnished confession

---

[3] ["The Sybarite: A Guide to the Ruthless Enjoyment of Life."—TRANS.]

of a type of this sort, and the book seems to me worth reading on that account alone.

On the lower levels, this type is the lover of tangible reality, with little inclination for reflection and no desire to dominate. To feel the object, to have sensations and if possible enjoy them—that is his constant aim. He is by no means unlovable; on the contrary, his lively capacity for enjoyment makes him very good company; he is usually a jolly fellow, and sometimes a refined aesthete. In the former case the great problems of life hang on a good or indifferent dinner; in the latter, it's all a question of good taste. Once an object has given him a sensation, nothing more remains to be said or done about it. It cannot be anything except concrete and real; conjectures that go beyond the concrete are admitted only on condition that they enhance sensation. The intensification does not necessarily have to be pleasurable, for this type need not be a common voluptuary; he is merely desirous of the strongest sensations, and these, by his very nature, he can receive only from outside. What comes from inside seems to him morbid and suspect. He always reduces his thoughts and feelings to objective causes, to influences emanating from objects, quite unperturbed by the most glaring violations of logic. Once he can get back to tangible reality in any form he can breathe again. In this respect he is surprisingly credulous. He will unhesitatingly connect a psychogenic symptom with a drop in the barometer, while on the other hand the existence of a psychic conflict seems to him morbid imagination. His love is unquestionably rooted in the physical attractions of its object. If normal, he is conspicuously well adjusted to reality. That is his ideal, and it even makes him considerate of others. As he has no ideals connected with ideas, he has no reason to act in any way contrary to the reality of things as they are. This manifests itself in all the externals of his life. He dresses well, as befits the occasion; he keeps a good table with plenty of drink for his friends, making them feel very grand, or at least giving them to understand that his refined taste entitles him to make a few demands of them. He may even convince them that certain sacrifices are decidedly worth while for the sake of style.

The more sensation predominates, however, so that the subject disappears behind the sensation, the less agreeable does this type become. He develops into a crude pleasure-seeker, or else degenerates into an unscrupulous, effete aesthete. Although the object has become quite indispensable to him, yet, as something existing in its own right, it is none the less devalued. It is ruthlessly exploited and squeezed dry, since now its sole use is to stimulate sensation. The bondage to the object is carried to the extreme limit. In consequence, the unconscious is forced out of its compensatory role into open opposition. Above all, the repressed intuitions begin to assert themselves in the form of projections. The wildest suspicions arise; if the object is a sexual one, jealous fantasies and anxiety states gain the upper hand. More acute cases develop every sort of phobia, and, in particular, compulsion symptoms. The pathological contents have a markedly unreal character, with a frequent moral or religious streak. A pettifogging captiousness follows, or a grotesquely punctilious morality combined with primitive, "magical" superstitions that fall back on abstruse rites. All these things have their source in the repressed inferior functions which have been driven into harsh opposition to the conscious attitude, and they appear in a guise that is all the more striking because they rest on the most absurd assumptions, in complete contrast to the conscious sense of reality. The whole structure of thought and feeling seems, in this second personality, to be twisted into a pathological parody: reason turns into hair-splitting pedantry, morality into dreary moralizing and blatant Pharisaism, religion into ridiculous superstition, and intuition, the noblest gift of man, into meddlesome officiousness, poking into every corner; instead of gazing into the far distance, it descends to the lowest level of human meanness.

The specifically compulsive character of the neurotic symptoms is the unconscious counterpart of the easy-going attitude of the pure sensation type, who, from the standpoint of rational judgment, accepts indiscriminately everything that happens. Although this does not by any means imply an absolute lawlessness and lack of restraint, it nevertheless deprives him of the essential restraining power of judgment. But rational judgment is a conscious coercion which the rational type appears to impose on himself of his own free will. This coercion overtakes the sensation type from the unconscious, in the form of compulsion. Moreover, the very existence of a judgment means that the rational type's relation to the object will never become an absolute tie, as it is in the case of the sensation type. When his attitude attains an abnormal degree of one-sidedness, therefore, he is in danger of being overpowered by the unconscious in the same measure as he is consciously in the grip of the object. If he should become neurotic, it is much harder to treat him by rational means because the functions which the analyst must turn to are in a relatively undifferentiated state, and little or no reliance can be placed on them. Special techniques for bringing emotional pressure to bear are often needed in order to make him at all conscious.

Intuition

In the extraverted attitude, intuition as the function of unconscious perception is wholly directed to external objects. Because intuition is in the main an unconscious process, its nature is very difficult to grasp. The intuitive function is represented in consciousness by an attitude of expectancy, by vision and penetration; but only from the subsequent result can it be established how much of what was "seen" was actually in the object, and how much was "read into" it. Just as sensation, when it is the dominant function, is not a mere reactive process of no further significance for the object, but an activity that seizes and shapes its object, so intuition is not mere perception, or vision, but an active, creative process that puts into the object just as much as it takes out. Since it does this unconsciously, it also has an unconscious effect on the object.

The primary function of intuition, however, is simply to transmit images, or perceptions of relations between things, which could not be transmitted by the other functions or only in a very roundabout way. These images have the value of specific insights which have a decisive influence on action whenever intuition is given priority. In this case, psychic adaptation will be grounded almost entirely on intuitions. Thinking, feeling, and sensation are then largely repressed, sensation being the one most affected, because, as the conscious sense function, it offers the greatest obstacle to intuition. Sensation is a hindrance to clear, unbiased, naïve perception; its intrusive sensory stimuli direct attention to the physical surface, to the very things round and beyond which intuition tries to peer. But since extraverted intuition is directed predominantly to objects, it actually comes very close to sensation; indeed, the expectant attitude to external objects is just as likely to make use of sensation. Hence, if intuition is to function properly, sensation must to a large extent be suppressed. By sensation I mean in this instance the simple and immediate sense-impression understood as a clearly defined physiological and psychic datum. This must be expressly established beforehand because, if I ask an intuitive how he orients himself, he will speak of things that are almost indistinguishable from sense-impressions. Very often he will even use the word "sensation." He does have sensations, of course, but he is not guided by them as such; he uses them merely as starting-points for his perceptions. He selects them by unconscious predilection. It is not the strongest sensation, in the physiological sense, that is accorded the chief value, but any sensation whatsoever whose value is enhanced by the intuitive's unconscious attitude. In this way it may eventually come to acquire the chief value, and to his conscious mind it appears to be pure sensation. But actually it is not so.

Just as extraverted sensation strives to reach the highest pitch of actuality, because this alone can give the appearance of a full life, so intuition tries to apprehend the widest range of *possibilities*, since only through envisioning possibilities is intuition fully satisfied. It seeks to discover what possibilities the objective situation holds in store; hence, as a subordinate function (i.e., when not in the position of priority), it is the auxiliary that automatically comes into play when no other function can find a way out of a hopelessly blocked situation. When it is the dominant function, every ordinary situation in life seems like a locked room which intuition has to open. It is constantly seeking fresh outlets and new possibilities in external life. In a very short time every existing situation becomes a prison for the intuitive, a chain that has to be broken. For a time objects appear to have an exaggerated value, if they should serve to bring about a solution, a deliverance, or lead to the discovery of a new possibility. Yet no sooner have they served their purpose as stepping-stones or bridges than they lose their value altogether and are discarded as burdensome appendages. Facts are acknowledged only if they open new possibilities of advancing beyond them and delivering the individual from their power. Nascent possibilities are compelling motives from which intuition cannot escape and to which all else must be sacrificed.

The Extraverted Intuitive Type

Whenever intuition predominates, a peculiar and unmistakable psychology results. Because extraverted intuition is oriented by the object, there is a marked dependence on external situations, but it is altogether different from the dependence of the sensation type. The intuitive is never to be found in the world of accepted reality-values, but he has a keen nose for anything new and in the making. Because he is always seeking out new possibilities, stable conditions suffocate him. He seizes on new objects or situations with great intensity, sometimes with extraordinary enthusiasm, only to abandon them cold-bloodedly, without any compunction and apparently without remembering them, as soon as their range is known and no further developments can be divined. So long as a new possibility is in the offing, the intuitive is bound to it with the shackles of fate. It is as though his whole life vanished in the new situation. One gets the impression, which he himself shares, that he has always just reached a final turning-point, and that from now on he can think and feel nothing else. No matter how reasonable and suitable it may be, and although every conceivable argument speaks for its stability, a day will come when nothing will deter him from regarding as a prison the very situation that seemed to promise him freedom and deliverance, and from acting accordingly. Neither reason nor feeling can restrain him or frighten him away from a new possibility, even though it goes against all his previous convictions. Thinking and feeling, the indispensable components of conviction, are his inferior functions, carrying no weight and hence incapable of effectively withstanding the power of intuition. And yet these functions are the only ones that could compensate its supremacy by supplying the *judgment* which the intuitive type totally lacks. The intuitive's morality is governed neither by thinking nor by feeling; he has his own characteristic morality, which consists in a loyalty to his vision and in voluntary submission to its authority. Consideration for the welfare of others is weak. Their psychic well-being counts as little with him as does his own. He has equally little regard for their convictions and way of life, and on this account he is often put down as an immoral and unscrupulous adventurer. Since his intuition is concerned with externals and with ferreting out their possibilities, he readily turns to professions in which he can exploit these capacities to the full. Many business tycoons, entrepreneurs, speculators, stockbrokers, politicians, etc., belong to this type. It would seem to be more common among women, however, than among men. In women the intuitive capacity shows itself not so much in the professional as in the social sphere. Such women understand the art of exploiting every social occasion, they make the right social connections, they seek out men with prospects only to abandon everything again for the sake of a new possibility.

It goes without saying that such a type is uncommonly important both economically and culturally. If his intentions are good, i.e., if his attitude is not too egocentric, he can render exceptional service as the initiator or promoter of new enterprises. He is the natural champion of all minorities with a future. Because he is able, when oriented more to people than things, to make an intuitive diagnosis of their abilities and potentialities, he can also "make" men. His capacity to inspire courage or to kindle enthusiasm for anything new is unrivalled, although he may already have dropped it by the morrow. The stronger his intuition, the more his ego becomes fused with all the possibilities he envisions. He brings his vision to life, he presents it convincingly and with dramatic fire, he embodies it, so to speak. But this is not play-acting, it is a kind of fate.

Naturally this attitude holds great dangers, for all too easily the intuitive may fritter away his life on things and people, spreading about him an abundance of life which others live and not he himself. If only he could stay put, he would reap the fruits of his labours; but always he must be running after a new possibility, quitting his newly planted fields while others gather in the harvest. In the end he goes away empty. But when the intuitive lets things come to such a pass, he also has his own unconscious against him. The unconscious of the intuitive bears some resemblance to that of the sensation type.

Thinking and feeling, being largely repressed, come up with infantile, archaic thoughts and feelings similar to those of the countertype. They take the form of intense projections which are just as absurd as his, though they seem to lack the "magical" character of the latter and are chiefly concerned with quasi-realities such as sexual suspicions, financial hazards, forebodings of illness, etc. The difference seems to be due to the repression of real sensations. These make themselves felt when, for instance, the intuitive suddenly finds himself entangled with a highly unsuitable woman—or, in the case of a woman, with an unsuitable man—because these persons have stirred up the archaic sensations. This leads to an unconscious, compulsive tie which bodes nobody any good. Cases of this kind are themselves symptomatic of compulsion, to which the intuitive is as prone as the sensation type. He claims a similar freedom and exemption from restraint, submitting his decisions to no rational judgment and relying entirely on his nose for the possibilities that chance throws in his way. He exempts himself from the restrictions of reason only to fall victim to neurotic compulsions in the form of over-subtle ratiocinations, hair-splitting dialectics, and a compulsive tie to the sensation aroused by the object. His conscious attitude towards both sensation and object is one of ruthless superiority. Not that he means to be ruthless or superior—he simply does not see the object that everyone else sees and rides roughshod over it, just as the sensation type has no eyes for its soul. But sooner or later the object takes revenge in the form of compulsive hypochondriacal ideas, phobias, and every imaginable kind of absurd bodily sensation.

Summary of the Extraverted Irrational Types

I call the two preceding types irrational for the reasons previously discussed, namely that whatever they do or do not do is based not on rational judgment but on the sheer intensity of perception. Their perception is directed simply and solely to events as they happen, no selection being made by judgment. In this respect they have a decided advantage over the two judging types. Objective events both conform to law and are accidental. In so far as they conform to law, they are accessible to reason; in so far as they are accidental, they are not.

Conversely, we might also say that an event conforms to law when it presents an aspect accessible to reason, and that when it presents an aspect for which we can find no law we call it accidental. The postulate of universal lawfulness is a postulate of reason alone, but in no sense is it a postulate of our perceptive functions. Since these are in no way based on the principle of reason and its postulates, they are by their very nature irrational. That is why I call the perception types "irrational" by nature. But merely because they subordinate judgment to perception, it would be quite wrong to regard them as "unreasonable." It would be truer to say that they are in the highest degree *empirical*. They base themselves exclusively on experience—so exclusively that, as a rule, their judgment cannot keep pace with their experience. But the judging functions are none the less present, although they eke out a largely unconscious existence. Since the unconscious, in spite of its separation from the conscious subject, is always appearing on the scene, we notice in the actual life of the irrational types striking judgments and acts of choice, but they take the form of apparent sophistries, cold-hearted criticisms, and a seemingly calculating choice of persons and situations. These traits have a rather infantile and even primitive character; both types can on occasion be astonishingly naïve, as well as ruthless, brusque, and violent. To the rational types the real character of these people might well appear rationalistic and calculating in the worst sense. But this judgment would be valid only for their unconscious, and therefore quite incorrect for their conscious psychology, which is entirely oriented by perception, and because of its irrational nature is quite unintelligible to any rational judgment. To the rational mind it might even seem that such a hodge-podge of accidentals hardly deserves the name "psychology" at all. The irrational type ripostes with an equally contemptuous opinion of his opposite number: he sees him as something only half alive, whose sole aim is to fasten the fetters of reason on everything living and strangle it with judgments. These are crass extremes, but they nevertheless occur.

From the standpoint of the rational type, the other might easily be represented as an inferior kind of rationalist—when, that is to say, he is judged by what happens to him. For what happens to him is not accidental—here he is the master—

instead, the accidents that befall him take the form of rational judgments and rational intentions, and these are the things he stumbles over. To the rational mind this is something almost unthinkable, but its unthinkableness merely equals the astonishment of the irrational type when he comes up against someone who puts rational ideas above actual and living happenings. Such a thing seems to him scarcely credible. As a rule it is quite hopeless to discuss these things with him as questions of principle, for all rational communication is just as alien and repellent to him as it would be unthinkable for the rationalist to enter into a contract without mutual consultation and obligation.

This brings me to the problem of the psychic relationship between the two types. Following the terminology of the French school of hypnotists, psychic relationship is known in modern psychiatry as "rapport." Rapport consists essentially in a feeling of agreement in spite of acknowledged differences. Indeed, the recognition of existing differences, if it be mutual, is itself a rapport, a feeling of agreement. If in a given case we make this feeling conscious to a higher degree than usual, we discover that it is not just a feeling whose nature cannot be analysed further, but at the same time an insight or a content of cognition which presents the point of agreement in conceptual form. This rational presentation is valid only for the rational types, but not for the irrational, whose rapport is based not on judgment but on the parallelism of living events. His feeling of agreement comes from the common perception of a sensation or intuition. The rational type would say that rapport with the irrational depends purely on chance. If, by some accident, the objective situations are exactly in tune, something like a human relationship takes place, but nobody can tell how valid it is or how long it will last. To the rational type it is often a painful thought that the relationship will last just as long as external circumstances and chance provide a common interest. This does not seem to him particularly human, whereas it is precisely in this that the irrational type sees a human situation of particular beauty. The result is that each regards the other as a man destitute of relationships, who cannot be relied upon, and with whom one can never get on decent terms. This unhappy outcome, however, is reached only when one makes a conscious effort to assess the nature of one's relationships with others. But since this kind of psychological conscientiousness is not very common, it frequently happens that despite an absolute difference of standpoint a rapport nevertheless comes about, and in the following way: one party, by unspoken projection, assumes that the other is, in all essentials, of the same opinion as himself, while the other divines or senses an objective community of interest, of which, however, the former has no conscious inkling and whose existence he would at once dispute, just as it would never occur to the other that his relationship should be based on a common point of view. A rapport of this kind is by far the most frequent; it rests on mutual projection, which later becomes the source of many misunderstandings.

Psychic relationship, in the extraverted attitude, is always governed by objective factors and external determinants. What a man is within himself is never of any decisive significance. For our present-day culture the extraverted attitude to the problem of human relationships is the principle that counts; naturally the introverted principle occurs too, but it is still the exception and has to appeal to the tolerance of the age.

3. THE INTROVERTED TYPE

a. The General Attitude of Consciousness

As I have already explained in the previous section, the introvert is distinguished from the extravert by the fact that he does not, like the latter, orient himself by the object and by objective data, but by subjective factors. I also mentioned[4] that the introvert interposes a subjective view between the perception of the object and his own action, which prevents the action from assuming a character that fits the objective situation. Naturally this is a special instance, mentioned by way of example and intended to serve only as a simple illustration. We must now attempt a formulation on a broader basis.

Although the introverted consciousness is naturally aware of external conditions, it selects the subjective determinants as

[4]Supra, p. 4–5.

the decisive ones. It is therefore oriented by the factor in perception and cognition which responds to the sense stimulus in accordance with the individual's subjective disposition. For example, two people see the same object, but they never see it in such a way that the images they receive are absolutely identical. Quite apart from the variable acuteness of the sense organs and the personal equation, there often exists a radical difference, both in kind and in degree, in the psychic assimilation of the perceptual image. Whereas the extravert continually appeals to what comes to him from the object, the introvert relies principally on what the sense impression constellates in the subject. The difference in the case of a single apperception may, of course, be very delicate, but in the total psychic economy it makes itself felt in the highest degree, particularly in the effect it has on the ego. If I may anticipate, I consider the viewpoint which inclines, with Weininger, to describe the introverted attitude as philautic, autoerotic, egocentric, subjectivistic, egotistic, etc., to be misleading in principle and thoroughly depreciatory. It reflects the normal bias of the extraverted attitude in regard to the nature of the introvert. We must not forget—although the extravert is only too prone to do so—that perception and cognition are not purely objective, but are also subjectively conditioned. The world exists not merely in itself, but also as it appears to me. Indeed, at bottom, we have absolutely no criterion that could help us to form a judgment of a world which was unassimilable by the subject. If we were to ignore the subjective factor, it would be a complete denial of the great doubt as to the possibility of absolute cognition. And this would mean a relapse into the stale and hollow positivism that marred the turn of the century—an attitude of intellectual arrogance accompanied by crudeness of feeling, a violation of life as stupid as it is presumptuous. By overvaluing our capacity for objective cognition we repress the importance of the subjective factor, which simply means a denial of the subject. But what is the subject? The subject is man himself—we are the subject. Only a sick mind could forget that cognition must have a subject, and that there is no knowledge whatever and therefore no world at all unless "I know" has been said, though with this statement one has already expressed the subjective limitation of all knowledge.

This applies to all the psychic functions: they have a subject which is just as indispensable as the object. It is characteristic of our present extraverted sense of values that the word "subjective" usually sounds like a reproof; at all events the epithet "merely subjective" is brandished like a weapon over the head of anyone who is not boundlessly convinced of the absolute superiority of the object. We must therefore be quite clear as to what "subjective" means in this inquiry. By the subjective factor I understand that psychological action or reaction which merges with the effect produced by the object and so gives rise to a new psychic datum. In so far as the subjective factor has, from the earliest times and among all peoples, remained in large measure constant, elementary perceptions and cognitions being almost universally the same, it is a reality that is just as firmly established as the external object. If this were not so, any sort of permanent and essentially unchanging reality would be simply inconceivable, and any understanding of the past would be impossible. In this sense, therefore, the subjective factor is as ineluctable a datum as the extent of the sea and the radius of the earth. By the same token, the subjective factor has all the value of a co-determinant of the world we live in, a factor that can on no account be left out of our calculations. It is another universal law, and whoever bases himself on it has a foundation as secure, as permanent, and as valid as the man who relies on the object. But just as the object and objective data do not remain permanently the same, being perishable and subject to chance, so too the subjective factor is subject to variation and individual hazards. For this reason its value is also merely relative. That is to say, the excessive development of the introverted standpoint does not lead to a better and sounder use of the subjective factor, but rather to an artificial subjectivizing of consciousness which can hardly escape the reproach "merely subjective." This is then counterbalanced by a de-subjectivization which takes the form of an exaggerated extraverted attitude, an attitude aptly described by Weininger as "misautic." But since the introverted attitude is based on the ever-present, extremely real, and absolutely indispensable fact of psychic adaptation, expressions like "philautic," "egocentric," and so on are out of place and objectionable because they arouse the prejudice that it is always a question of the beloved ego. Nothing could be more mistaken than such an assumption. Yet one is continually meeting it in the judgments of the extravert on the introvert. Not, of course, that I wish to ascribe this error to individual extraverts; it is rather to be put down to the generally accepted extraverted view which is by no means restricted to the extraverted type, for it has just as many representatives among introverts, very much to their own detriment. The reproach of being untrue to their own nature can justly be levelled at the latter, whereas this at least cannot be held against the former.

The introverted attitude is normally oriented by the psychic structure, which is in principle hereditary and is inborn in the subject. This must not be assumed, however, to be simply identical with the subject's ego, as is implied by the above designations of Weininger; it is rather the psychic structure of the subject prior to any ego-development. The really fundamental subject, the self, is far more comprehensive than the ego, since the former includes the unconscious whereas the latter is essentially the focal point of consciousness. Were the ego identical with the self, it would be inconceivable how we could sometimes see ourselves in dreams in quite different forms and with entirely different meanings. But it is a characteristic peculiarity of the introvert, which is as much in keeping with his own inclination as with the general bias, to confuse his ego with the self, and to exalt it as the subject of the psychic process, thus bringing about the aforementioned subjectivization of consciousness which alienates him from the object.

The psychic structure is the same as what Semon calls "mneme"[5] and what I call the "collective unconscious." The individual self is a portion or segment or representative of something present in all living creatures, an exponent of the specific mode of psychological behaviour, which varies from species to species and is inborn in each of its members. The inborn mode of *acting* has long been known as *instinct*, and for the inborn mode of psychic apprehension I have proposed the term *archetype*.[6] I may assume that what is understood by in-

---

[5] *Die Mneme als erhaltendes Prinzip im Wechsel des organischen Geschehens* (trans. by L. Simon: *The Mneme*).

[6] "Instinct and the Unconscious," pars. 270ff.

stinct is familiar to everyone. It is another matter with the archetype. What I understand by it is identical with the "primordial image," a term borrowed from Jacob Burckhardt,[7] and I describe it as such in the Definitions that conclude this book. I must here refer the reader to the definition "Image."[8]

The archetype is a symbolic formula which always begins to function when there are no conscious ideas present, or when conscious ideas are inhibited for internal or external reasons. The contents of the collective unconscious are represented in consciousness in the form of pronounced preferences and definite ways of looking at things. These subjective tendencies and views are generally regarded by the individual as being determined by the object—incorrectly, since they have their source in the unconscious structure of the psyche and are merely released by the effect of the object. They are stronger than the object's influence, their psychic value is higher, so that they superimpose themselves on all impressions. Thus, just as it seems incomprehensible to the introvert that the object should always be the decisive factor, it remains an enigma to the extravert how a subjective standpoint can be superior to the objective situation. He inevitably comes to the conclusion that the introvert is either a conceited egoist or crack-brained bigot. Today he would be suspected of harbouring an unconscious power-complex. The introvert certainly lays himself open to these suspicions, for his positive, highly generalizing manner of expression, which appears to rule out every other opinion from the start, lends countenance to all the extravert's prejudices. Moreover the inflexibility of his subjective judgment, setting itself above all objective data, is sufficient in itself to create the impression of marked egocentricity. Faced with this prejudice the introvert is usually at a loss for the right argument, for he is quite unaware of the unconscious but generally quite valid assumptions on which his subjective judgment and his subjective perceptions are based. In the fashion of the times he looks outside for an answer, instead of seeking it behind his own consciousness. Should he become neurotic, it is the sign of an almost complete identity of the ego with the self; the importance of the self is reduced to nil, while the ego

[7][Cf. *Symbols of Transformation*, par. 45, n. 45.—EDITORS.]
[8][See pp. 113ff.—EDITORS.]

48

is inflated beyond measure. The whole world-creating force of the subjective factor becomes concentrated in the ego, producing a boundless power-complex and a fatuous egocentricity. Every psychology which reduces the essence of man to the unconscious power drive springs from this kind of disposition. Many of Nietzsche's lapses in taste, for example, are due to this subjectivization of consciousness.

b. *The Attitude of the Unconscious*

The predominance of the subjective factor in consciousness naturally involves a devaluation of the object. The object is not given the importance that belongs to it by right. Just as it plays too great a role in the extraverted attitude, it has too little meaning for the introvert. To the extent that his consciousness is subjectivized and excessive importance attached to the ego, the object is put in a position which in the end becomes untenable. The object is a factor whose power cannot be denied, whereas the ego is a very limited and fragile thing. It would be a very different matter if the self opposed the object. Self and world are commensurable factors; hence a normal introverted attitude is as justifiable and valid as a normal extraverted attitude. But if the ego has usurped the claims of the subject, this naturally produces, by way of compensation, an unconscious reinforcement of the influence of the object. In spite of positively convulsive efforts to ensure the superiority of the ego, the object comes to exert an overwhelming influence, which is all the more invincible because it seizes on the individual unawares and forcibly obtrudes itself on his consciousness. As a result of the ego's unadapted relation to the object—for a desire to dominate it is not adaptation—a compensatory relation arises in the unconscious which makes itself felt as an absolute and irrepressible tie to the object. The more the ego struggles to preserve its independence, freedom from obligation, and superiority, the more it becomes enslaved to the objective data. The individual's freedom of mind is fettered by the ignominy of his financial dependence, his freedom of action trembles in the face of public opinion, his moral superiority collapses in a morass of inferior relationships, and his desire to dominate ends in a pitiful craving to be loved. It is now the unconscious that takes care of the relation to the object, and it does so in a way that is calculated to bring the illusion of power and the fantasy of superiority to utter ruin. The object assumes terrifying proportions in spite of the conscious attempt to degrade it. In consequence, the ego's efforts to detach itself from the object and get it under control become all the more violent. In the end it surrounds itself with a regular system of defences (aptly described by Adler) for the purpose of preserving at least the illusion of superiority. The introvert's alienation from the object is now complete; he wears himself out with defence measures on the one hand, while on the other he makes fruitless attempts to impose his will on the object and assert himself. These efforts are constantly being frustrated by the overwhelming impressions received from the object. It continually imposes itself on him against his will, it arouses in him the most disagreeable and intractable affects and persecutes him at every step. A tremendous inner struggle is needed all the time in order to "keep going." The typical form his neurosis takes is psychasthenia, a malady characterized on the one hand by extreme sensitivity and on the other by great proneness to exhaustion and chronic fatigue.

An analysis of the personal unconscious reveals a mass of power fantasies coupled with fear of objects which he himself has forcibly activated, and of which he is often enough the victim. His fear of objects develops into a peculiar kind of cowardliness; he shrinks from making himself or his opinions felt, fearing that this will only increase the object's power. He is terrified of strong affects in others, and is hardly ever free from the dread of falling under hostile influences. Objects possess puissant and terrifying qualities for him—qualities he cannot consciously discern in them, but which he imagines he sees through his unconscious perception. As his relation to the object is very largely repressed, it takes place via the unconscious, where it becomes charged with the latter's qualities. These qualities are mostly infantile and archaic, so that the relation to the object becomes primitive too, and the object seems endowed with magical powers. Anything strange and new arouses fear and mistrust, as though concealing unknown perils; heirlooms and suchlike are attached to his soul as by invisible threads; any change is upsetting, if not positively dangerous, as it seems to denote a magical animation of the object. His ideal is a lonely island where nothing moves except what he permits to move. Vischer's novel, *Auch Einer*, affords deep insight into this side of the introvert's psychology, and also into the underlying symbolism of the collective unconscious. But this latter question I must leave to one side, since it is not specific to a description of types but is a general phenomenon.

c. The Peculiarities of the Basic Psychological Functions in the Introverted Attitude

Thinking

In the section on extraverted thinking I gave a brief description of introverted thinking (pars. 578–79) and must refer to it again here. Introverted thinking is primarily oriented by the subjective factor. At the very least the subjective factor expresses itself as a feeling of guidance which ultimately determines judgment. Sometimes it appears as a more or less complete image which serves as a criterion. But whether introverted thinking is concerned with concrete or with abstract objects, always at the decisive points it is oriented by subjective data. It does not lead from concrete experience back again to the object, but always to the subjective content. External facts are not the aim and origin of this thinking, though the introvert would often like to make his thinking appear so. It begins with the subject and leads back to the subject, far though it may range into the realm of actual reality. With regard to the establishment of new facts it is only indirectly of value, since new views rather than knowledge of new facts are its main concern. It formulates questions and creates theories, it opens up new prospects and insights, but with regard to facts its attitude is one of reserve. They are all very well as illustrative examples, but they must not be allowed to predominate. Facts are collected as evidence for a theory, never for their own sake. If ever this happens, it is merely a concession to the extraverted style. Facts are of secondary importance for this kind of thinking; what seems to it of paramount importance is the development and presentation of the subjective idea, of the initial symbolic image hovering darkly before the mind's eye.

Its aim is never an intellectual reconstruction of the concrete fact, but a shaping of that dark image into a luminous idea. It wants to reach reality, to see how the external fact will fit into and fill the framework of the idea, and the creative power of this thinking shows itself when it actually creates an idea which, though not inherent in the concrete fact, is yet the most suitable abstract expression of it. Its task is completed when the idea it has fashioned seems to emerge so inevitably from the external facts that they actually prove its validity.

But no more than extraverted thinking can wrest a sound empirical concept from concrete facts or create new ones can introverted thinking translate the initial image into an idea adequately adapted to the facts. For, as in the former case the purely empirical accumulation of facts paralyzes thought and smothers their meaning, so in the latter case introverted thinking shows a dangerous tendency to force the facts into the shape of its image, or to ignore them altogether in order to give fantasy free play. In that event it will be impossible for the finished product—the idea—to repudiate its derivation from the dim archaic image. It will have a mythological streak which one is apt to interpret as "originality" or, in more pronounced cases, as mere whimsicality, since its archaic character is not immediately apparent to specialists unfamiliar with mythological motifs. The subjective power of conviction exerted by an idea of this kind is usually very great, and it is all the greater the less it comes into contact with external facts. Although it may seem to the originator of the idea that his meagre store of facts is the actual source of its truth and validity, in reality this is not so, for the idea derives its convincing power from the unconscious archetype, which, as such, is eternally valid and true. But this truth is so universal and so symbolic that it must first be assimilated to the recognized and recognizable knowledge of the time before it can become a practical truth of any value for life. What would causality be, for instance, if it could nowhere be recognized in practical causes and practical effects?

This kind of thinking easily gets lost in the immense truth of the subjective factor. It creates theories for their own sake, apparently with an eye to real or at least possible facts, but always with a distinct tendency to slip over from the world of ideas into mere imagery. Accordingly, visions of numerous possibilities appear on the scene, but none of them ever becomes a reality, until finally images are produced which no longer express anything externally real, being mere symbols of the ineffable and unknowable. It is now merely a mystical thinking and quite as unfruitful as thinking that remains bound to objective data. Whereas the latter sinks to the level of a mere representation of facts, the former evaporates into a representation of the irrepresentable, far beyond anything that could be expressed in an image. The representation of facts has an incontestable truth because the subjective factor is excluded and the facts speak for themselves. Similarly, the representation of the irrepresentable has an immediate, subjective power of conviction because it demonstrates its own existence. The one says "Est, ergo est"; the other says "Cogito, ergo cogito." Introverted thinking carried to extremes arrives at the evidence of its own subjective existence, and extraverted thinking at the evidence of its complete identity with the objective fact. Just as the latter abnegates itself by evaporating into the object, the former empties itself of each and every content and has to be satisfied with merely existing. In both cases the further development of life is crowded out of the thinking function into the domain of the other psychic functions, which till then had existed in a state of relative unconsciousness. The extraordinary impoverishment of introverted thinking is compensated by a wealth of unconscious facts. The more consciousness is impelled by the thinking function to confine itself within the smallest and emptiest circle—which seems, however, to contain all the riches of the gods—the more the unconscious fantasies will be enriched by a multitude of archaic contents, a veritable "pandaemonium" of irrational and magical figures, whose physiognomy will accord with the nature of the function that will supersede the thinking function as the vehicle of life. If it should be the intuitive function, then the "other side" will be viewed through the eyes of a Kubin or a Meyrink.[9] If it is the feeling function, then quite unheard-of and fantastic feeling relationships will be formed, coupled with contradictory and unintelligible value judgments. If it is the sensation function, the

[9] Kubin, *The Other Side*, and Meyrink, *Das grüne Gesicht*.

senses will nose up something new, and never experienced before, in and outside the body. Closer examination of these permutations will easily demonstrate a recrudescence of primitive psychology with all its characteristic features. Naturally, such experiences are not merely primitive, they are also symbolic; in fact, the more primordial and aboriginal they are, the more they represent a future truth. For everything old in the unconscious hints at something coming.

Under ordinary circumstances, not even the attempt to get to the "other side" will be successful—and still less the redeeming journey through the unconscious. The passage across is usually blocked by conscious resistance to any subjection of the ego to the realities of the unconscious and their determining power. It is a state of dissociation, in other words a neurosis characterized by inner debility and increasing cerebral exhaustion—the symptoms of psychasthenia.

The Introverted Thinking Type

Just as we might take Darwin as an example of the normal extraverted thinking type, the normal introverted thinking type could be represented by Kant. The one speaks with facts, the other relies on the subjective factor. Darwin ranges over the wide field of objective reality. Kant restricts himself to a critique of knowledge. Cuvier and Nietzsche would form an even sharper contrast.

The introverted thinking type is characterized by the primacy of the kind of thinking I have just described. Like his extraverted counterpart, he is strongly influenced by ideas, though his ideas have their origin not in objective data but in his subjective foundation. He will follow his ideas like the extravert, but in the reverse direction: inwards and not outwards. Intensity is his aim, not extensity. In these fundamental respects he differs quite unmistakably from his extraverted counterpart. What distinguishes the other, namely his intense relation to objects, is almost completely lacking in him as in every introverted type. If the object is a person, this person has a distinct feeling that he matters only in a negative way; in milder cases he is merely conscious of being *de trop*, but with a more extreme type he feels himself warded off as something definitely disturbing. This negative relation to the object, ranging from indifference to aversion, characterizes every introvert and makes a description of the type exceedingly difficult. Everything about him tends to disappear and get concealed. His judgment appears cold, inflexible, arbitrary, and ruthless, because it relates far less to the object than to the subject. One can feel nothing in it that might possibly confer a higher value on the object; it always bypasses the object and leaves one with a feeling of the subject's superiority. He may be polite, amiable, and kind, but one is constantly aware of a certain uneasiness betraying an ulterior motive—the disarming of an opponent, who must at all costs be pacified and placated lest he prove himself a nuisance. In no sense, of course, is he an opponent, but if he is at all sensitive he will feel himself repulsed, and even belittled.

Invariably the object has to submit to a certain amount of neglect, and in pathological cases it is even surrounded with quite unnecessary precautionary measures. Thus this type tends to vanish behind a cloud of misunderstanding, which gets all the thicker the more he attempts to assume, by way of compensation and with the help of his inferior functions, an air of urbanity which contrasts glaringly with his real nature. Although he will shrink from no danger in building up his world of ideas, and never shrinks from thinking a thought because it might prove to be dangerous, subversive, heretical, or wounding to other people's feelings, he is none the less beset by the greatest anxiety if ever he has to make it an objective reality. That goes against the grain. And when he does put his ideas into the world, he never introduces them like a mother solicitous for her children, but simply dumps them there and gets extremely annoyed if they fail to thrive on their own account. His amazing unpracticalness and horror of publicity in any form have a hand in this. If in his eyes his product appears correct and true, then it must be so in practice, and others have got to bow to its truth. Hardly ever will he go out of his way to win anyone's appreciation of it, especially anyone of influence. And if ever he brings himself to do so, he generally sets about it so clumsily that it has just the opposite of the effect intended. He usually has bad experiences with rivals in his own field because he never understands how to curry their favour; as a rule he only succeeds in showing them how entirely superfluous they are to him. In the pursuit of his ideas he is generally stubborn, headstrong, and quite unamenable to influence. His suggestibility to personal influences is in strange contrast to this. He has only to be convinced of a person's seeming innocuousness to lay himself open to the most undesirable elements. They seize hold of him from the unconscious. He lets himself be brutalized and exploited in the most ignominious way if only he can be left in peace to pursue his ideas. He simply does not see when he is being plundered behind his back and wronged in practice, for to him the relation to people and things is secondary and the objective evaluation of his product is something he remains unconscious of. Because he thinks out his problems to the limit, he complicates them and constantly gets entangled in his own scruples and misgivings. However clear to him the inner structure of his thoughts may be, he is not in the least clear where or how they link up with the world of reality. Only with the greatest difficulty will he bring himself to admit that what is clear to him may not be equally clear to everyone. His style is cluttered with all sorts of adjuncts, accessories, qualifications, retractions, saving clauses, doubts, etc., which all come from his scrupulosity. His work goes slowly and with difficulty.

In his personal relations he is taciturn or else throws himself on people who cannot understand him, and for him this is one more proof of the abysmal stupidity of man. If for once he is understood, he easily succumbs to credulous overestimation of his prowess. Ambitious women have only to know how to take advantage of his cluelessness in practical matters to make an easy prey of him; or he may develop into a misanthropic bachelor with a childlike heart. Often he is gauche in his behaviour, painfully anxious to escape notice, or else remarkably unconcerned and childishly naïve. In his own special field of work he provokes the most violent opposition, which he has no notion how to deal with, unless he happens to be seduced by his primitive affects into acrimonious and fruitless polemics. Casual acquaintances think him inconsiderate and domineering. But the better one knows him, the more favourable one's judgment becomes, and his closest friends value his intimacy very highly. To outsiders he seems prickly, unapproachable, and arrogant, and sometimes soured as a result of his antisocial prejudices. As a personal teacher he has little influence, since the mentality of his students is strange to him. Besides, teaching has, at bottom, no interest for him unless it happens to provide him with a theoretical problem. He is a poor teacher, because all the time he is teaching his thought is occupied with the material itself and not with its presentation.

With the intensification of his type, his convictions become all the more rigid and unbending. Outside influences are shut off; as a person, too, he becomes more unsympathetic to his wider circle of acquaintances, and therefore more dependent on his intimates. His tone becomes personal and surly, and though his ideas may gain in profundity they can no longer be adequately expressed in the material at hand. To compensate for this, he falls back on emotionality and touchiness. The outside influences he has brusquely fended off attack him from within, from the unconscious, and in his efforts to defend himself he attacks things that to outsiders seem utterly unimportant. Because of the subjectivization of consciousness resulting from his lack of relationship to the object, what secretly concerns his own person now seems to him of extreme importance. He begins to confuse his subjective truth with his own personality. Although he will not try to press his convictions on anyone personally, he will burst out with vicious, personal retorts against every criticism, however just. Thus his isolation gradually increases. His originally fertilizing ideas become destructive, poisoned by the sediment of bitterness. His struggle against the influences emanating from the unconscious increases with his external isolation, until finally they begin to cripple him. He thinks his withdrawal into ever-increasing solitude will protect him from the unconscious influences, but as a rule it only plunges him deeper into the conflict that is destroying him from within.

The thinking of the introverted type is positive and synthetic in developing ideas which approximate more and more to the eternal validity of the primordial images. But as their connection with objective experience becomes more and more tenuous, they take on a mythological colouring and no longer hold true for the contemporary situation. Hence his thinking is of value for his contemporaries only so long as it is manifestly and intelligibly related to the known facts of the time.

Once it has become mythological, it ceases to be relevant and runs on in itself. The counterbalancing functions of feeling, intuition, and sensation are comparatively unconscious and inferior, and therefore have a primitive extraverted character that accounts for all the troublesome influences from outside to which the introverted thinker is prone. The various protective devices and psychological minefields which such people surround themselves with are known to everyone, and I can spare myself a description of them. They all serve as a defence against "magical" influences—and among them is a vague fear of the feminine sex.

Feeling

Introverted feeling is determined principally by the subjective factor. It differs quite as essentially from extraverted feeling as introverted from extraverted thinking. It is extremely difficult to give an intellectual account of the introverted feeling process, or even an approximate description of it, although the peculiar nature of this kind of feeling is very noticeable once one has become aware of it. Since it is conditioned subjectively and is only secondarily concerned with the object, it seldom appears on the surface and is generally misunderstood. It is a feeling which seems to devalue the object, and it therefore manifests itself for the most part negatively. The existence of positive feeling can be inferred only indirectly. Its aim is not to adjust itself to the object, but to subordinate it in an unconscious effort to realize the underlying images. It is continually seeking an image which has no existence in reality, but which it has seen in a kind of vision. It glides unheedingly over all objects that do not fit in with its aim. It strives after inner intensity, for which the objects serve at most as a stimulus. The depth of this feeling can only be guessed—it can never be clearly grasped. It makes people silent and difficult of access; it shrinks back like a violet from the brute nature of the object in order to fill the depths of the subject. It comes out with negative judgments or assumes an air of profound indifference as a means of defence.

The primordial images are, of course, just as much ideas as feelings. Fundamental ideas, ideas like God, freedom, and immortality, are just as much feeling-values as they are significant ideas. Everything, therefore, that we have said about introverted thinking is equally true of introverted feeling, only here everything is felt while there it was thought. But the very fact that thoughts can generally be expressed more intelligibly than feelings demands a more than ordinary descriptive or artistic ability before the real wealth of this feeling can be even approximately presented or communicated to the world. If subjective thinking can be understood only with difficulty because of its unrelatedness, this is true in even higher degree of subjective feeling. In order to communicate with others, it has to find an external form not only acceptable to itself, but capable also of arousing a parallel feeling in them. Thanks to the relatively great inner (as well as outer) uniformity of human beings, it is actually possible to do this, though the form acceptable to feeling is extraordinarily difficult to find so long as it is still mainly oriented to the fathomless store of primordial images. If, however, feeling is falsified by an egocentric attitude, it at once becomes unsympathetic, because it is then concerned mainly with the ego. It inevitably creates the impression of sentimental self-love, of trying to make itself interesting, and even of morbid self-admiration. Just as the subjectivized consciousness of the introverted thinker, striving after abstraction to the nth degree, only succeeds in intensifying a thought-process that is in itself empty, the intensification of egocentric feeling only leads to inane transports of feeling for their own sake. This is the mystical, ecstatic stage which opens the way for the extraverted functions that feeling has repressed. Just as introverted thinking is counterbalanced by a primitive feeling, to which objects attach themselves with magical force, introverted feeling is counterbalanced by a primitive thinking, whose concretism and slavery to facts surpass all bounds. Feeling progressively emancipates itself from the object and creates for itself a freedom of action and conscience that is purely subjective, and may even renounce all traditional values. But so much the more does unconscious thinking fall a victim to the power of objective reality.

The Introverted Feeling Type

It is principally among women that I have found the predominance of introverted feeling. "Still waters run deep" is very true of such women. They are mostly silent, inaccessible, hard to understand; often they hide behind a childish or banal mask, and their temperament is inclined to melancholy. They neither shine nor reveal themselves. As they are mainly guided by their subjective feelings, their true motives generally remain hidden. Their outward demeanour is harmonious, inconspicuous, giving an impression of pleasing repose, or of sympathetic response, with no desire to affect others, to impress, influence, or change them in any way. If this outward aspect is more pronounced, it arouses a suspicion of indifference and coldness, which may actually turn into a disregard for the comfort and well-being of others. One is distinctly aware then of the movement of feeling away from the object. With the normal type, however, this happens only when the influence of the object is too strong. The feeling of harmony, therefore, lasts only so long as the object goes its own moderate way and makes no attempt to cross the other's path. There is little effort to respond to the real emotions of the other person; they are more often damped down and rebuffed, or cooled off by a negative value judgment. Although there is a constant readiness for peaceful and harmonious co-existence, strangers are shown no touch of amiability, no gleam of responsive warmth, but are met with apparent indifference or a repelling coldness. Often they are made to feel entirely superfluous. Faced with anything that might carry her away or arouse enthusiasm, this type observes a benevolent though critical neutrality, coupled with a faint trace of superiority that soon takes the wind out of the sails of a sensitive person. Any stormy emotion, however, will be struck down with murderous coldness, unless it happens to catch the woman on her unconscious side—that is, unless it hits 'her feelings by arousing a primordial image. In that case she simply feels paralysed for the moment, and this in due course invariably produces an even more obstinate resistance which will hit the other person in his most vulnerable spot. As far as possible, the feeling relationship is kept to the safe middle path, all intemperate passions being resolutely tabooed. Expressions of feeling therefore remain niggardly, and the other person has a permanent sense of being undervalued once he becomes conscious of it. But this need not always be so, because very often he remains unconscious of the lack of feeling shown to him, in which case the unconscious demands of feeling will produce symptoms designed to compel attention.

Since this type appears rather cold and reserved, it might seem on a superficial view that such women have no feelings at all. But this would be quite wrong; the truth is, their feelings are intensive rather than extensive. They develop in depth. While an extensive feeling of sympathy can express itself in appropriate words and deeds, and thus quickly gets back to normal again, an intensive sympathy, being shut off from every means of expression, acquires a passionate depth that comprises a whole world of misery and simply gets benumbed. It may perhaps break out in some extravagant form and lead to an astounding act of an almost heroic character, quite unrelated either to the subject herself or to the object that provoked the outburst. To the outside world, or to the blind eyes of the extravert, this intensive sympathy looks like coldness, because usually it does nothing visible, and an extraverted consciousness is unable to believe in invisible forces. Such a misunderstanding is a common occurrence in the life of this type, and is used as a weighty argument against the possibility of any deeper feeling relation with the object. But the real object of this feeling is only dimly divined by the normal type herself. It may express itself in a secret religiosity anxiously guarded from profane eyes, or in intimate poetic forms that are kept equally well hidden, not without the secret ambition of displaying some kind of superiority over the other person by this means. Women often express a good deal of their feelings through their children, letting their passion flow secretly into them.

Although this tendency to overpower or coerce the other person with her secret feelings rarely plays a disturbing role in the normal type, and never leads to a serious attempt of this kind, some trace of it nevertheless seeps through into the personal effect they have on him, in the form of a domineering influence often difficult to define. It is sensed as a sort of stifling or oppressive feeling which holds everybody around her under a spell. It gives a woman of this type a mysterious power that may prove terribly fascinating to the extraverted man, for it touches his unconscious. This power comes from the deeply felt, unconscious images, but consciously she is apt to relate it to the ego, whereupon her influence becomes debased into a personal tyranny. Whenever the unconscious subject is identified with the ego, the mysterious power of intensive feeling turns into a banal and overweening desire to dominate, into vanity and despotic bossiness. This produces a type of woman notorious for her unscrupulous ambition and mischievous cruelty. It is a change, however, that leads to neurosis.

So long as the ego feels subordinate to the unconscious subject, and feeling is aware of something higher and mightier than the ego, the type is normal. Although the unconscious thinking is archaic, its reductive tendencies help to compensate the occasional fits of trying to exalt the ego into the subject. If this should nevertheless happen as a result of complete suppression of the counterbalancing subliminal processes, the unconscious thinking goes over into open opposition and gets projected. The egocentrized subject now comes to feel the power and importance of the devalued object. She begins consciously to feel "what other people think." Naturally, other people are thinking all sorts of mean things, scheming evil, contriving plots, secret intrigues, etc. In order to forestall them, she herself is obliged to start counter-intrigues, to suspect others and sound them out, and weave counterplots. Beset by rumours, she must make frantic efforts to get her own back and be top dog. Endless clandestine rivalries spring up, and in these embittered struggles she will shrink from no baseness or meanness, and will even prostitute her virtues in order to play the trump card. Such a state of affairs must end in exhaustion. The form of neurosis is neurasthenic rather than hysterical, often with severe physical complications, such as anaemia and its sequelae.

Summary of the Introverted Rational Types

Both the foregoing types may be termed rational, since they are grounded on the functions of rational judgment. Rational judgment is based not merely on objective but also on subjective data. The predominance of one or the other factor, however, as a result of a psychic disposition often existing from early youth, will give the judgment a corresponding bias. A judgment that is truly rational will appeal to the objective and the subjective factor equally and do justice to both. But that would be an ideal case and would presuppose an equal development of both extraversion and introversion. In practice, however, either movement excludes the other, and, so long as this dilemma remains, they cannot exist side by side but at best successively. Under ordinary conditions, therefore, an ideal rationality is impossible. The rationality of a rational type always has a typical bias. Thus, the judgment of the introverted rational types is undoubtedly rational, only it is oriented more by the subjective factor. This does not necessarily imply any logical bias, since the bias lies in the premise. The premise consists in the predominance of the subjective factor prior to all conclusions and judgments. The superior value of the subjective as compared with the objective factor appears self-evident from the beginning. It is not a question of *assigning* this value, but, as we have said, of a natural disposition existing before all rational valuation. Hence, to the introvert, rational judgment has many nuances which differentiate it from that of the extravert. To mention only the most general instance, the chain of reasoning that leads to the subjective factor seems to the introvert somewhat more rational than the one that leads to the object. This difference, though slight and practically unnoticeable in individual cases, builds up in the end to unbridgeable discrepancies which are the more irritating the less one is aware of the minimal shift of standpoint occasioned by the psychological premise. A capital error regularly creeps in here, for instead of recognizing the difference in the premise one tries to demonstrate a fallacy in the conclusion. This recognition is a difficult matter for every rational type, since it undermines the apparently absolute validity of his own principle and delivers him over to its antithesis, which for him amounts to a catastrophe.

The introvert is far more subject to misunderstanding than the extravert, not so much because the extravert is a more merciless or critical adversary than he himself might be, but because the style of the times which he himself imitates works against him. He finds himself in the minority, not in numerical relation to the extravert, but in relation to the general Western view of the world as judged by his feeling. In so far as he is a convinced participator in the general style, he undermines his own foundations; for the general style, acknowledging as it does only the visible and tangible values, is opposed to his specific principle. Because of its invisibility, he is obliged to depreciate the subjective factor, and must force himself to join in the extraverted overvaluation of the object. He himself sets the subjective factor at too low a value, and his feelings of inferiority are his chastisement for this sin. Little wonder, therefore, that it is precisely in the present epoch, and particularly in those movements which are somewhat ahead of the time, that the subjective factor reveals itself in exaggerated, tasteless forms of expression bordering on caricature. I refer to the art of the present day.

The undervaluation of his own principle makes the introvert egotistical and forces on him the psychology of the underdog. The more egotistical he becomes, the more it seems to him that the others, who are apparently able, without qualms, to conform to the general style, are the oppressors against whom he must defend himself. He generally does not see that his chief error lies in not depending on the subjective factor with the same trust and devotion with which the extravert relies on the object. His undervaluation of his own principle makes his leanings towards egotism unavoidable, and because of this he fully deserves the censure of the extravert. If he remained true to his own principle, the charge of egotism would be altogether false, for his attitude would be justified by its effects in general, and the misunderstanding would be dissipated.

Sensation

Sensation, which by its very nature is dependent on the object and on objective stimuli, undergoes considerable modification in the introverted attitude. It, too, has a subjective factor, for besides the sensed object there is a sensing subject who adds his subjective disposition to the objective stimulus. In the introverted attitude sensation is based predominantly on the subjective component of perception. What I mean by this is best illustrated by works of art which reproduce external objects. If, for instance, several painters were to paint the same landscape, each trying to reproduce it faithfully, each painting will be different from the others, not merely because of differences in ability, but chiefly because of different ways of seeing; indeed, in some of the paintings there will be a distinct psychic difference in mood and the treatment of colour and form. These qualities betray the influence of the subjective factor. The subjective factor in sensation is essentially the same as in the other functions we have discussed. It is an unconscious disposition which alters the sense-perception at its source, thus depriving it of the character of a purely objective influence. In this case, sensation is related primarily to the subject and only secondarily to the object. How extraordinarily strong the subjective factor can be is shown most clearly in art. Its predominance sometimes amounts to a complete suppression of the object's influence, and yet the sensation remains sensation even though it has become a perception of the subjective factor and the object has sunk to the level of a mere stimulus. Introverted sensation is oriented accordingly. True sense-perception certainly exists, but it always looks as though the object did not penetrate into the subject in its own right, but as though the subject were seeing it quite differently, or saw quite other things than other people see. Actually, he perceives the same things as everybody else, only he does not stop at the purely objective influence, but concerns himself with the subjective perception excited by the objective stimulus.

Subjective perception is markedly different from the objective. What is perceived is either not found at all in the object, or is, at most, merely suggested by it. That is, although the perception can be similar to that of other men, it is not immediately derived from the objective behaviour of things. It does not impress one as a mere product of consciousness—it is too genuine for that. But it makes a definite psychic impression because elements of a higher psychic order are discernible in it. This order, however, does not coincide with the contents of consciousness. It has to do with presuppositions or dispositions of the collective unconscious, with mythological images, with primordial possibilities of ideas. Subjective perception is characterized by the meaning that clings to it. It means more than the mere image of the object, though naturally only to one for whom the subjective factor means anything at all. To another, the reproduced subjective impression seems to suffer from the defect of not being sufficiently like the object and therefore to have failed in its purpose.

65

Introverted sensation apprehends the background of the physical world rather than its surface. The decisive thing is not the reality of the object, but the reality of the subjective factor, of the primordial images which, in their totality, constitute a psychic mirror-world. It is a mirror with the peculiar faculty of reflecting the existing contents of consciousness not in their known and customary form but, as it were, *sub specie aeternitatis*, somewhat as a million-year-old consciousness might see them. Such a consciousness would see the becoming and passing away of things simultaneously with their momentary existence in the present, and not only that, it would also see what was before their becoming and will be after their passing hence. Naturally this is only a figure of speech, but one that I needed in order to illustrate in some way the peculiar nature of introverted sensation. We could say that introverted sensation transmits an image which does not so much reproduce the object as spread over it the patina of age-old subjective experience and the shimmer of events still unborn. The bare sense impression develops in depth, reaching into the past and future, while extraverted sensation seizes on the momentary existence of things open to the light of day.

The Introverted Sensation Type

The predominance of introverted sensation produces a definite type, which is characterized by certain peculiarities. It is an irrational type, because it is oriented amid the flux of events not by rational judgment but simply by what happens. Whereas the extraverted sensation type is guided by the intensity of objective influences, the introverted type is guided by the intensity of the subjective sensation excited by the objective stimulus. Obviously, therefore, no proportional relation exists between object and sensation, but one that is apparently quite unpredictable and arbitrary. What will make an impression and what will not can never be seen in advance, and from outside. Did there exist an aptitude for expression in any way proportional to the intensity of his sensations, the irrationality of this type would be extraordinarily striking. This is the case, for instance, when an individual is a creative artist. But since this is the exception, the introvert's characteristic difficulty in expressing himself also conceals his irrationality. On the contrary, he may be conspicuous for his calmness and passivity, or for his rational self-control. This peculiarity, which often leads a superficial judgment astray, is really due to his unrelatedness to objects. Normally the object is not consciously devalued in the least, but its stimulus is removed from it and immediately replaced by a subjective reaction no longer related to the reality of the object. This naturally has the same effect as devaluation. Such a type can easily make one question why one should exist at all, or why objects in general should have any justification for their existence since everything essential still goes on happening without them. This doubt may be justified in extreme cases, but not in the normal, since the objective stimulus is absolutely necessary to sensation and merely produces something different from what the external situation might lead one to expect.

Seen from the outside, it looks as though the effect of the object did not penetrate into the subject at all. This impression is correct inasmuch as a subjective content does, in fact, intervene from the unconscious and intercept the effect of the object. The intervention may be so abrupt that the individual appears to be shielding himself directly from all objective influences. In more serious cases, such a protective defence actually does exist. Even with only a slight increase in the power of the unconscious, the subjective component of sensation becomes so alive that it almost completely obscures the influence of the object. If the object is a person, he feels completely devalued, while the subject has an illusory conception of reality, which in pathological cases goes so far that he is no longer able to distinguish between the real object and the subjective perception. Although so vital a distinction reaches the vanishing point only in near-psychotic states, yet long before that the subjective perception can influence thought, feeling, and action to an excessive degree despite the fact that the object is clearly seen in all its reality. When its influence does succeed in penetrating into the subject—because of its special intensity or because of its complete analogy with the unconscious image— even the normal type will be compelled to *act* in accordance with the unconscious model. Such action has an illusory character unrelated to objective reality and is extremely disconcerting. It instantly reveals the reality-alienating subjectivity of this type. But when the influence of the object does not break through completely, it is met with well-intentioned neutrality, disclosing little sympathy yet constantly striving to soothe and adjust. The too low is raised a little, the too high is lowered, enthusiasm is damped down, extravagance restrained, and anything out of the ordinary reduced to the right formula—all this in order to keep the influence of the object within the necessary bounds. In this way the type becomes a menace to his environment because his total innocuousness is not altogether above suspicion. In that case he easily becomes a victim of the aggressiveness and domineeringness of others. Such men allow themselves to be abused and then take their revenge on the most unsuitable occasions with redoubled obtuseness and stubbornness.

If no capacity for artistic expression is present, all impressions sink into the depths and hold consciousness under a spell, so that it becomes impossible to master their fascination by giving them conscious expression. In general, this type can organize his impressions only in archaic ways, because thinking and feeling are relatively unconscious and, if conscious at all, have at their disposal only the most necessary, banal, everyday means of expression. As conscious functions, they are wholly incapable of adequately reproducing his subjective perceptions. This type, therefore, is uncommonly inaccessible to objective understanding, and he usually fares no better in understanding himself.

Above all, his development alienates him from the reality of the object, leaving him at the mercy of his subjective perceptions, which orient his consciousness to an archaic reality, although his lack of comparative judgment keeps him wholly unconscious of this fact. Actually he lives in a mythological world, where men, animals, locomotives, houses, rivers, and mountains appear either as benevolent deities or as malevolent demons. That they appear thus to him never enters his head, though that is just the effect they have on his judgments and actions. He judges and acts as though he had such powers to deal with; but this begins to strike him only when he discovers that his sensations are totally different from reality. If he has any aptitude for objective reason, he will sense this difference as morbid; but if he remains faithful to his irrationality, and is ready to grant his sensations reality value, the objective world will appear a mere make-believe and a comedy. Only in extreme cases, however, is this dilemma reached. As a rule he resigns himself to his isolation and the banality of the world, which he has unconsciously made archaic.

His unconscious is distinguished chiefly by the repression of intuition, which consequently acquires an extraverted and archaic character. Whereas true extraverted intuition is possessed of a singular resourcefulness, a "good nose" for objectively real possibilities, this archaicized intuition has an amazing flair for all the ambiguous, shadowy, sordid, dangerous possibilities lurking in the background. The real and conscious intentions of the object mean nothing to it; instead, it sniffs out every conceivable archaic motive underlying such an intention. It therefore has a dangerous and destructive quality that contrasts glaringly with the well-meaning innocuousness of the conscious attitude. So long as the individual does not hold too aloof from the object, his unconscious intuition has a salutary compensating effect on the rather fantastic and overcredulous attitude of consciousness. But as soon as the unconscious becomes antagonistic, the archaic intuitions come to the surface and exert their pernicious influence, forcing themselves on the individual and producing compulsive ideas of the most perverse kind. The result is usually a compulsion neurosis, in which the hysterical features are masked by symptoms of exhaustion.

Intuition

Introverted intuition is directed to the inner object, a term that might justly be applied to the contents of the unconscious. The relation of inner objects to consciousness is entirely analogous to that of outer objects, though their reality is not physical but psychic. They appear to intuitive perception as subjective images of things which, though not to be met with in the outside world, constitute the contents of the unconscious, and of the collective unconscious in particular. These contents *per se* are naturally not accessible to experience, a quality they have in common with external objects. For just as external objects correspond only relatively to our perception of them, so the phenomenal forms of the inner objects are also relative—products of their (to us) inaccessible essence and of the peculiar nature of the intuitive function.

Like sensation, intuition has its subjective factor, which is suppressed as much as possible in the extraverted attitude but is the decisive factor in the intuition of the introvert. Although his intuition may be stimulated by external objects, it does not concern itself with external possibilities but with what the external object has released within him. Whereas introverted sensation is mainly restricted to the perception, via the unconscious, of the phenomena of innervation and is arrested there, introverted intuition suppresses this side of the subjective factor and perceives the image that caused the innervation. Supposing, for instance, a man is overtaken by an attack of psychogenic vertigo. Sensation is arrested by the peculiar nature of this disturbance of innervation, perceiving all its qualities, its intensity, its course, how it arose and how it passed, but not advancing beyond that to its content, to the thing that caused the disturbance. Intuition, on the other hand, receives from sensation only the impetus to its own immediate activity; it peers behind the scenes, quickly perceiving the inner image that gave rise to this particular form of expression—the attack of vertigo. It sees the image of a tottering man pierced through the heart by an arrow. This image fascinates the intuitive activity; it is arrested by it, and seeks to explore every detail of it. It holds fast to the vision, observing with the liveliest interest how the picture changes, unfolds, and finally fades.

In this way introverted intuition perceives all the background processes of consciousness with almost the same distinctness as extraverted sensation registers external objects. For intuition, therefore, unconscious images acquire the dignity of things. But, because intuition excludes the co-operation of sensation, it obtains little or no knowledge of the disturbances of innervation or of the physical effects produced by the unconscious images. The images appear as though detached from the subject, as though existing in themselves without any relation to him. Consequently, in the above-mentioned example, the introverted intuitive, if attacked by vertigo, would never imagine that the image he perceived might in some way refer to himself. To a judging type this naturally seems almost inconceivable, but it is none the less a fact which I have often come across in my dealings with intuitives.

The remarkable indifference of the extraverted intuitive to external objects is shared by the introverted intuitive in relation to inner objects. Just as the extraverted intuitive is continually scenting out new possibilities, which he pursues with equal unconcern for his own welfare and for that of others, pressing on quite heedless of human considerations and tearing down what has just been built in his everlasting search for change, so the introverted intuitive moves from image to image, chasing after every possibility in the teeming womb of the unconscious, without establishing any connection between them and himself. Just as the world of appearances can never become a moral problem for the man who merely senses it, the world of inner images is never a moral problem for the intuitive. For both of them it is an aesthetic problem, a matter of perception, a "sensation." Because of this, the introverted intuitive has little consciousness of his own bodily existence or of its effect on others. The extravert would say: "Reality does not exist for him, he gives himself up to fruitless fantasies." The perception of the images of the unconscious, produced in such inexhaustible abundance by the creative energy of life, is of course fruitless from the standpoint of immediate utility. But since these images represent possible views of the world which may give life a new potential, this function, which to the outside world is the strangest of all, is as indispensable to the total psychic economy as is the corresponding human type to the psychic life of a people. Had this type not existed, there would have been no prophets in Israel.

Introverted intuition apprehends the images arising from the *a priori* inherited foundations of the unconscious. These archetypes, whose innermost nature is inaccessible to experience, are the precipitate of the psychic functioning of the whole ancestral line; the accumulated experiences of organic life in general, a million times repeated, and condensed into types. In these archetypes, therefore, all experiences are represented which have happened on this planet since primeval times. The more frequent and the more intense they were, the more clearly focussed they become in the archetype. The archetype would thus be, to borrow from Kant, the noumenon of the image which intuition perceives and, in perceiving, creates.

Since the unconscious is not just something that lies there like a psychic *caput mortuum*, but coexists with us and is constantly undergoing transformations which are inwardly connected with the general run of events, introverted intuition, through its perception of these inner processes, can supply certain data which may be of the utmost importance for understanding what is going on in the world. It can even foresee new possibilities in more or less clear outline, as well as events which later actually do happen. Its prophetic foresight is explained by its relation to the archetypes, which represent the laws governing the course of all experienceable things.

The Introverted Intuitive Type

The peculiar nature of introverted intuition, if it gains the ascendency, produces a peculiar type of man: the mystical dreamer and seer on the one hand, the artist and the crank on the other. The artist might be regarded as the normal representative of this type, which tends to confine itself to the perceptive character of intuition. As a rule, the intuitive stops at perception; perception is his main problem, and—in the case of a creative artist—the shaping of his perception. But the crank is content with a visionary idea by which he himself is shaped and determined. Naturally the intensification of intuition often results in an extraordinary aloofness of the individual from tangible reality; he may even become a complete enigma to his immediate circle. If he is an artist, he reveals strange, far-off things in his art, shimmering in all colours, at once portentous and banal, beautiful and grotesque, sublime and whimsical. If not an artist, he is frequently a misunderstood genius, a great man "gone wrong," a sort of wise simpleton, a figure for "psychological" novels.

Although the intuitive type has little inclination to make a moral problem of perception, since a strengthening of the judging functions is required for this, only a slight differentiation of judgment is sufficient to shift intuitive perception from the purely aesthetic into the moral sphere. A variety of this type is thus produced which differs essentially from the aesthetic, although it is none the less characteristic of the introverted intuitive. The moral problem arises when the intuitive tries to relate himself to his vision, when he is no longer satisfied with mere perception and its aesthetic configuration and evaluation, when he confronts the questions: What does this mean for me or the world? What emerges from this vision in the way of a duty or a task, for me or the world? The pure intuitive who represses his judgment, or whose judgment is held in thrall by his perceptive faculties, never faces this question squarely, since his only problem is the "know-how" of perception. He finds the moral problem unintelligible or even absurd, and as far as possible forbids his thoughts to dwell on the disconcerting vision. It is different with the morally oriented intuitive. He reflects on the meaning of his vision, and is less concerned with developing its aesthetic possibilities than with the moral effects which emerge from its intrinsic significance. His judgment allows him to discern, though often only darkly, that he, as a man and a whole human being, is somehow involved in his vision, that it is not just an object to be perceived, but wants to participate in the life of the subject. Through this realization he feels bound to transform his vision into his own life. But since he tends to rely most predominantly on his vision, his moral efforts become one-sided; he makes himself and his life symbolic—adapted, it is true, to the inner and eternal meaning of events, but unadapted to present-day reality. He thus deprives himself of any influence upon it because he remains uncomprehended. His language is not the one currently spoken—it has become too subjective. His arguments lack the convincing power of reason. He can only profess or proclaim. His is "the voice of one crying in the wilderness."

What the introverted intuitive represses most of all is the sensation of the object, and this colours his whole unconscious. It gives rise to a compensatory extraverted sensation function of an archaic character. The unconscious personality can best be described as an extraverted sensation type of a rather low and primitive order. Instinctuality and intemperance are the hallmarks of this sensation, combined with an extraordinary dependence on sense-impressions. This compensates the rarefied air of the intuitive's conscious attitude, giving it a certain weight, so that complete "sublimation" is prevented. But if, through a forced exaggeration of the conscious attitude, there should be a complete subordination to inner perceptions, the unconscious goes over to the opposition, giving rise to compulsive sensations whose excessive dependence on the object directly contradicts the conscious attitude. The form of neurosis is a compulsion neurosis with hypochondriacal symptoms, hypersensitivity of the sense organs, and compulsive ties to particular persons or objects.

Summary of the Introverted Irrational Types

The two types just described are almost inaccessible to judgment from outside. Being introverted, and having in consequence little capacity or desire for expression, they offer but a frail handle in this respect. As their main activity is directed inwards, nothing is outwardly visible but reserve, secretiveness, lack of sympathy, uncertainty, and an apparently groundless embarrassment. When anything does come to the surface, it is generally an indirect manifestation of the inferior and relatively unconscious functions. Such manifestations naturally arouse all the current prejudices against this type. Accordingly they are mostly underestimated, or at least misunderstood. To the extent that they do not understand themselves—because they very largely lack judgment—they are also powerless to understand why they are so constantly underestimated by the public. They cannot see that their efforts to be forthcoming are, as a matter of fact, of an inferior character. Their vision is enthralled by the richness of subjective events. What is going on inside them is so captivating, and of such inexhaustible charm, that they simply do not notice that the little they do manage to communicate contains hardly anything of what they themselves have experienced. The fragmentary and episodic character of their communications makes too great a demand on the understanding and good will of those around them; also, their communications are without the personal warmth that alone carries the power of conviction. On the contrary, these types have very often a harsh, repelling manner, though of this they are quite unaware and did not intend it. We shall form a fairer judgment of such people, and show them greater forbearance, when we begin to realize how hard it is to translate into intelligible language what is perceived within. Yet this forbearance must not go so far as to exempt them altogether from the need to communicate. This would only do them the greatest harm. Fate itself prepares for them, perhaps even more than for other men, overwhelming external difficulties which have a very sobering effect on those intoxicated by the inner vision. Often it is only an intense personal need that can wring from them a human confession.

From an extraverted and rationalistic standpoint, these types are indeed the most useless of men. But, viewed from a higher standpoint, they are living evidence that this rich and varied world with its overflowing and intoxicating life is not purely external, but also exists within. These types are admittedly one-sided specimens of nature, but they are an object-lesson for the man who refuses to be blinded by the intellectual fashion of the day. In their own way, they are educators and promoters of culture. Their life teaches more than their words. From their lives, and not least from their greatest fault—their inability to communicate—we may understand one of the greatest errors of our civilization, that is, the superstitious belief in verbal statements, the boundless overestimation of instruction by means of words and methods. A child certainly allows himself to be impressed by the grand talk of his parents, but do they really imagine he is educated by it? Actually it is the parents' lives that educate the child—what they add by word and gesture at best serves only to confuse him. The same holds good for the teacher. But we have such a belief in method that, if only the method be good, the practice of it seems to sanctify the teacher. An inferior man is never a good teacher. But he can conceal his pernicious inferiority, which secretly poisons the pupil, behind an excellent method or an equally brilliant gift of gab. Naturally the pupil of riper years desires nothing better than the knowledge of useful methods, because he is already defeated by the general attitude, which believes in the all-conquering method. He has learned that the emptiest head, correctly parroting a method, is the best pupil. His whole environment is an optical demonstration that all success and all happiness are outside, and that only the right method is needed to attain the haven of one's desires. Or does, perchance, the life of his religious instructor demonstrate the happiness which radiates from the treasure of the inner vision? The irrational introverted types are certainly no teachers of a more perfect humanity; they lack reason and the ethics of reason. But their lives teach the other possibility, the interior life which is so painfully wanting in our civilization.

d. The Principal and Auxiliary Functions

In the foregoing descriptions I have no desire to give my readers the impression that these types occur at all frequently in such pure form in actual life. They are, as it were, only Galtonesque family portraits, which single out the common and therefore typical features, stressing them disproportionately, while the individual features are just as disproportionately effaced. Closer investigation shows with great regularity that, besides the most differentiated function, another, less differentiated function of secondary importance is invariably present in consciousness and exerts a co-determining influence.

To recapitulate for the sake of clarity: the products of all functions can be conscious, but we speak of the "consciousness" of a function only when its use is under the control of the will and, at the same time, its governing principle is the decisive one for the orientation of consciousness. This is true when, for instance, thinking is not a mere afterthought, or rumination, and when its conclusions possess an absolute validity, so that the logical result holds good both as a motive and as a guarantee of practical action without the backing of any further evidence. This absolute sovereignty always belongs, empirically, to one function alone, and *can* belong only to one function, because the equally independent intervention of another function would necessarily produce a different orientation which, partially at least, would contradict the first. But since it is a vital condition for the conscious process of adaptation always to have clear and unambiguous aims, the presence of a second function of equal power is naturally ruled out. This other function, therefore, can have only a secondary importance, as has been found to be the case in practice. Its secondary importance is due to the fact that it is not, like the primary function, valid in its own right as an absolutely reliable and decisive factor, but comes into play more as an auxiliary or complementary function. Naturally only those functions can appear as auxiliary whose nature is not opposed to the dominant function. For instance, feeling can never act as the second function alongside thinking, because it is by its very nature too strongly opposed to thinking. Thinking, if it is to be real thinking and true to its own principle, must rigorously exclude feeling. This, of course, does not do away with the fact that there are individuals whose thinking and feeling are on the same level, both being of equal motive power for consciousness. But in these cases there is also no question of a differentiated type, but merely of relatively undeveloped thinking and feeling. The uniformly conscious or uniformly unconscious state of the functions is, therefore, the mark of a primitive mentality.

Experience shows that the secondary function is always one whose nature is different from, though not antagonistic to, the primary function. Thus, thinking as the primary function can readily pair with intuition as the auxiliary, or indeed equally well with sensation, but, as already observed, never with feeling. Neither intuition nor sensation is antagonistic to thinking; they need not be absolutely excluded, for they are not of a nature equal and opposite to thinking, as feeling is—which, as a judging function, successfully competes with thinking—but are functions of perception, affording welcome assistance to thought. But as soon as they reached the same level of differentiation as thinking, they would bring about a change of attitude which would contradict the whole trend of thinking. They would change the judging attitude into a perceiving one; whereupon the principle of rationality indispensable to thought would be suppressed in favour of the irrationality of perception. Hence the auxiliary function is possible and useful only in so far as it *serves* the dominant function, without making any claim to the autonomy of its own principle.

For all the types met with in practice, the rule holds good that besides the conscious, primary function there is a relatively unconscious, auxiliary function which is in every respect different from the nature of the primary function. The resulting combinations present the familiar picture of, for instance, practical thinking allied with sensation, speculative thinking forging ahead with intuition, artistic intuition selecting and presenting its images with the help of feeling-values, philosophical intuition systematizing its vision into comprehensible thought by means of a powerful intellect, and so on.

The unconscious functions likewise group themselves in patterns correlated with the conscious ones. Thus, the correlative of conscious, practical thinking may be an unconscious, intuitive-feeling attitude, with feeling under a stronger inhibition than intuition. These peculiarities are of interest only for one who is concerned with the practical treatment of such cases, but it is important that he should know about them. I have frequently observed how an analyst, confronted with a terrific thinking type, for instance, will do his utmost to develop the feeling function directly out of the unconscious. Such an attempt is foredoomed to failure, because it involves too great a violation of the conscious standpoint. Should the violation nevertheless be successful, a really compulsive dependence of the patient on the analyst ensues, a transference that can only be brutally terminated, because, having been left without a standpoint, the patient has made his standpoint the analyst. But the approach to the unconscious and to the most repressed function is disclosed, as it were, of its own accord, and with adequate protection of the conscious standpoint, when the way of development proceeds via the auxiliary function—in the case of a rational type via one of the irrational functions. This gives the patient a broader view of what is happening, and of what is possible, so that his consciousness is sufficiently protected against the inroads of the unconscious. Conversely, in order to cushion the impact of the unconscious, an irrational type needs a stronger development of the rational auxiliary function present in consciousness.

The unconscious functions exist in an archaic, animal state. Hence their symbolic appearance in dreams and fantasies is usually represented as the battle or encounter between two animals or monsters.

DEFINITIONS

It may perhaps seem superfluous that I should add to my text a chapter dealing solely with definitions. But ample experience has taught me that, in psychological works particularly, one cannot proceed too cautiously in regard to the concepts and terms one uses: for nowhere do such wide divergences of meaning occur as in the domain of psychology, creating only too frequently the most obstinate misunderstandings. This drawback is due not only to the fact that the science of psychology is still in its infancy; there is the further difficulty that the empirical material, the object of scientific investigation, cannot be displayed in concrete form, as it were, before the eyes of the reader. The psychological investigator is always finding himself obliged to make extensive use of an indirect method of description in order to present the reality he has observed. Only in so far as elementary facts are communicated which are amenable to quantitative measurement can there be any question of a direct presentation. But how much of the actual psychology of man can be experienced and observed as quantitatively measurable facts? Such facts do exist, and I believe I have shown in my association studies[1] that extremely complicated psychological facts are accessible to quantitative measurement. But anyone who has probed more deeply into the nature of psychology, demanding something more of it as a science than that it should confine itself within the narrow limits of the scientific method, will also have realized that an experimental method will never succeed in doing justice to the nature of the human psyche, nor will it ever project anything like a true picture of the more complex psychic phenomena.

But once we leave the domain of measurable facts we are dependent on *concepts*, which have now to take over the role

[1] *Studies in Word-Association.*

79

of measure and number. The precision which measure and number lend to the observed fact can be replaced only by the *precision of the concept*. Unfortunately, as every investigator and worker in this field knows only too well, current psychological concepts are so imprecise and so ambiguous that mutual understanding is practically impossible. One has only to take the concept "feeling," for instance, and try to visualize everything this concept comprises, to get some sort of notion of the variability and ambiguity of psychological concepts in general. And yet the concept of feeling does express something characteristic that, though not susceptible of quantitative measurement, nevertheless palpably exists. One simply cannot resign oneself, as Wundt does in his physiological psychology, to a mere denial of such essential and fundamental phenomena, and seek to replace them by elementary facts or to resolve them into such. In this way an essential part of psychology is thrown overboard.

In order to escape the ill consequences of this overvaluation of the scientific method, one is obliged to have recourse to well-defined concepts. But in order to arrive at such concepts, the collaboration of many workers would be needed, a sort of *consensus gentium*. Since this is not within the bounds of possibility at present, the individual investigator must at least try to give his concepts some fixity and precision, and this can best be done by discussing the meaning of the concepts he employs so that everyone is in a position to see what in fact he means by them.

To meet this need I now propose to discuss my principal psychological concepts in alphabetical order, and I would like the reader to refer to these explanations in case of doubt. It goes without saying that these definitions and explanations are merely intended to establish the sense in which I myself use the concepts; far be it from me to affirm that this use is in all circumstances the only possible one or the absolutely right one.

1. ABSTRACTION, as the word itself indicates, is the drawing out or singling out of a content (a meaning, a general characteristic, etc.) from a context made up of other elements whose combination into a whole is something unique or individual and therefore cannot be compared with anything else.

Singularity, uniqueness, and incomparability are obstacles to cognition; hence the other elements associated with a content that is felt to be the essential one are bound to appear irrelevant.

Abstraction, therefore, is a form of mental activity that frees this content from its association with the irrelevant elements by distinguishing it from them or, in other words, *differentiating* it (v. *Differentiation*). In its wider sense, everything is *abstract* that is separated from its association with elements that are felt to have no relevance to its meaning.

Abstraction is an activity pertaining to the psychological *functions* (q.v.) in general. There is an abstract *thinking*, just as there is abstract *feeling, sensation,* and *intuition* (qq. v.). Abstract thinking singles out the rational, logical qualities of a given content from its intellectually irrelevant components. Abstract feeling does the same with a content characterized by its feeling-values; similarly with sensation and intuition. Hence, not only are there abstract thoughts but also abstract feelings, the latter being defined by Sully as intellectual, aesthetic, and moral.[2] To these Nahlowsky adds all religious feelings.[3] Abstract feelings would, in my view, correspond to the "higher" or "ideal" feelings of Nahlowsky. I put abstract feelings on the same level as abstract thoughts. Abstract sensation would be aesthetic as opposed to sensuous *sensation* (q.v.), and abstract intuition would be symbolic as opposed to fantastic *intuition* (v. *Fantasy* and *Intuition*).

In this work I also associate abstraction with the awareness of the psycho-energic process it involves. When I take an abstract attitude to an object, I do not allow the object to affect me in its totality; I focus my attention on one part of it by excluding all the irrelevant parts. My aim is to disembarrass myself of the object as a singular and unique whole and to abstract only a portion of this whole. No doubt I am aware of the whole, but I do not immerse myself in this awareness; my interest does not flow into the whole, but draws back from it, pulling the abstracted portion into myself, into my conceptual world, which is already prepared or constellated for the purpose of abstracting a part of the object. (It is only because of

[2] Sully, *The Human Mind*, II, ch. 16.
[3] Nahlòwsky, *Das Gefühlsleben*, p. 48.

a subjective constellation of concepts that I am able to abstract from the object.) "Interest" I conceive as the energy or *libido* (q.v.) which I bestow on the object as a value, or which the object draws from me, maybe even against my will or unknown to myself. I visualize the process of abstraction as a withdrawal of libido from the object, as a backflow of value from the object into a subjective, abstract content. For me, therefore, abstraction amounts to an energic *devaluation of the object*. In other words, abstraction is an introverting movement of libido (v. *Introversion*).

I call an *attitude* (q.v.) *abstractive* when it is both introverting and at the same time *assimilates* (q.v.) a portion of the object, felt to be essential, to abstract contents already constellated in the subject. The more abstract a content is, the more it is *irrepresentable*. I subscribe to Kant's view that a concept gets more abstract "the more the differences of things are left out of it,"[4] in the sense that abstraction at its highest level detaches itself absolutely from the object, thereby attaining the extreme limit of irrepresentability. It is this pure "abstract" which I term an *idea* (q.v.). Conversely, an abstract that still possesses some degree of representability or plasticity is a *concrete* concept (v. *Concretism*).

2. AFFECT. By the term affect I mean a state of feeling characterized by marked physical innervation on the one hand and a peculiar disturbance of the ideational process on the other.[5] I use *emotion* as synonymous with affect. I distinguish —in contrast to Bleuler (v. *Affectivity*)—*feeling* (q.v.) from affect, in spite of the fact that the dividing line is fluid, since every feeling, after attaining a certain strength, releases physical innervations, thus becoming an affect. For practical reasons, however, it is advisable to distinguish affect from feeling, since feeling can be a voluntarily disposable function, whereas affect is usually not. Similarly, affect is clearly distinguished from feeling by quite perceptible physical innervations, while feeling for the most part lacks them, or else their intensity is so slight that they can be demonstrated only by the most delicate instruments, as in the case of psychogalvanic phenom-

---

4 Kant, *Logik*, I, par. 6. (*Werke*, ed. Cassirer, VIII, p. 403.)
5 Wundt, *Grundzüge der physiologischen Psychologie*, pp. 209ff.

ena.[6] Affect becomes cumulative through the sensation of the physical innervations released by it. This observation gave rise to the James-Lange theory of affect, which derives affect causally from physical innervations. As against this extreme view, I regard affect on the one hand as a psychic feeling-state and on the other as a physiological innervation-state, each of which has a cumulative, reciprocal effect on the other. That is to say, a component of sensation allies itself with the intensified feeling, so that the affect is approximated more to *sensation* (q.v.) and essentially differentiated from the feeling-state. Pronounced affects, i.e., affects accompanied by violent physical innervations, I do not assign to the province of feeling but to that of the sensation function.

3. AFFECTIVITY is a term coined by Bleuler. It designates and comprises "not only the affects proper, but also the slight feelings or feeling-tones of pain and pleasure."[7] Bleuler distinguishes affectivity from the sense-perceptions and physical sensations as well as from "feelings" that may be regarded as inner perception processes (e.g., the "feeling" of certainty, of probability, etc.) or vague thoughts or discernments.[8]

4. ANIMA/ANIMUS, v. SOUL; SOUL-IMAGE.

5. APPERCEPTION is a psychic process by which a new content is articulated with similar, already existing contents in such a way that it becomes understood, apprehended, or "clear."[9] We distinguish *active* from *passive* apperception. The first is a process by which the subject, of his own accord and from his own motives, consciously apprehends a new content with attention and assimilates it to other contents already constellated; the second is a process by which a new content forces itself upon consciousness either from without (through the senses) or from within (from the unconscious) and, as it were,

---

[6] Féré, "Note sur des modifications de la résistance électrique," pp. 217ff.; Veraguth, "Das psychogalvanische Reflexphänomen," pp. 387ff.; Binswanger, "On the Psychogalvanic Phenomenon in Association Experiments," in *Studies in Word-Association*, pp. 446ff.; Jung, "On the Psychophysical Relations of the Association Experiment."

[7] Bleuler, *Affektivität, Suggestibilität, Paranoia*, p. 6.

[8] Ibid., pp. 13f.

[9] Wundt, *Grundzüge der physiologischen Psychologie*, I, p. 322.

compels attention and enforces apprehension. In the first case the activity lies with the *ego* (q.v.); in the second, with the self-enforcing new content.

6. ARCHAISM is a term by which I designate the "oldness" of psychic contents or *functions* (q.v.). By this I do not mean qualities that are "archaistic" in the sense of being pseudo-antique or copied, as in later Roman sculpture or nineteenth-century Gothic, but qualities that have the character of *relics*. We may describe as archaic all psychological traits that exhibit the qualities of the primitive mentality. It is clear that archaism attaches primarily to the *fantasies* (q.v.) of the unconscious, i.e., to the products of unconscious fantasy activity which reach consciousness. An *image* (q.v.) has an archaic quality when it possesses unmistakable mythological parallels.[10] Archaic, too, are the associations-by-analogy of unconscious fantasy, and so is their symbolism (v. *Symbol*). The relation of *identity* (q.v.) with an object, or *participation mystique* (q.v.), is likewise archaic. *Concretism* (q.v.) of thought and feeling is archaic; also compulsion and inability to control oneself (ecstatic or trance states, possession, etc.). Fusion of the psychological functions (v. *Differentiation*), of thinking with feeling, feeling with sensation, feeling with intuition, and so on, is archaic, as is also the fusion of part of a function with its counterpart, e.g., positive with negative feeling, or what Bleuler calls ambitendency and ambivalence, and such phenomena as *colour hearing*.

6a. ARCHETYPE,[11] v. IMAGE, primordial: also IDEA.

7. ASSIMILATION is the approximation of a new content of consciousness to already constellated subjective material,[12] the similarity of the new content to this material being especially accentuated in the process, often to the detriment of its independent qualities.[13] Fundamentally, assimilation is a process of *apperception* (q.v.), but is distinguished from apperception

[10] Jung, *Symbols of Transformation.*

[11] [Note by Editors of the *Gesammelte Werke*: "The structure of the archetype was always central to Jung's investigations, but the formulation of the concept took place only in the course of the years."] [For a helpful survey of the development of the concept, see Jacobi, *Complex/Archetype/Symbol.*—EDITORS.]

[12] Wundt, *Logik*, I, p. 23.

[13] Lipps, *Leitfaden der Psychologie*, p. 104.

by this element of approximation to the subjective material. It is in this sense that Wundt says:[14]

This way of building up ideas [i.e., by assimilation] is most conspicuous when the assimilating elements arise through reproduction, and the assimilated ones through an immediate sense impression. For then the elements of memory-images are projected, as it were, into the external object, so that, particularly when the object and the reproduced elements differ substantially from one another, the finished sense impression appears as an illusion, deceiving us as to the real nature of things.

I use the term assimilation in a somewhat broader sense, as the approximation of object to subject in general, and with it I contrast *dissimilation*, as the approximation of subject to object, and a consequent alienation of the subject from himself in favour of the object, whether it be an external object or a "psychological" object, for instance an idea.

8. ATTITUDE. This concept is a relatively recent addition to psychology. It originated with Müller and Schumann.[15] Whereas Külpe[16] defines attitude as a predisposition of the sensory or motor centres to react to a particular stimulus or constant impulse, Ebbinghaus[17] conceives it in a wider sense as an effect of training which introduces the factor of habit into individual acts that deviate from the habitual. Our use of the concept derives from Ebbinghaus's. For us, attitude is a readiness of the psyche to act or react in a certain way. The concept is of particular importance for the psychology of complex psychic processes because it expresses the peculiar fact that certain stimuli have too strong an effect on some occasions, and little or no effect on others. To have an attitude means to be ready for something definite, even though this something is unconscious; for having an attitude is synonymous with an *a priori* orientation to a definite thing, no matter whether this be represented in consciousness or not. The state of readiness, which I conceive attitude to be, consists in the presence of a

[14] Wundt, *Grundzüge*, III, p. 529.
[15] "Ueber die psychologischen Grundlagen der Vergleichung gehobener Gewichte," pp. 37ff.
[16] *Grundriss der Psychologie*, p. 44.
[17] *Grundzüge der Psychologie*, I, pp. 681f.

certain subjective constellation, a definite combination of psychic factors or contents, which will either determine action in this or that definite direction, or react to an external stimulus in a definite way. Active *apperception* (q.v.) is impossible without an attitude. An attitude always has a point of reference; this can be either conscious or unconscious, for in the act of apperceiving a new content an already constellated combination of contents will inevitably accentuate those qualities or elements that appear to belong to the subjective content. Hence a selection or judgment takes place which excludes anything irrelevant. As to what is or is not relevant, this is decided by the already constellated combination of contents. Whether the point of reference is conscious or unconscious does not affect the selectivity of the attitude, since the selection is implicit in the attitude and takes place automatically. It is useful, however, to distinguish between the two, because the presence of two attitudes is extremely frequent, one conscious and the other unconscious. This means that consciousness has a constellation of contents different from that of the unconscious, a duality particularly evident in neurosis.

The concept of attitude has some affinity with Wundt's concept of *apperception*, with the difference that apperception includes the process of relating the already constellated contents to the new content to be apperceived, whereas attitude relates exclusively to the subjectively constellated content. Apperception is, as it were, the bridge which connects the already existing, constellated contents with the new one, whereas attitude would be the support or abutment of the bridge on the one bank, and the new content the abutment on the other bank. Attitude signifies *expectation*, and expectation always operates selectively and with a sense of direction. The presence of a strongly feeling-toned content in the conscious field of vision forms (maybe with other contents) a particular constellation that is equivalent to a definite attitude, because such a content promotes the perception and apperception of everything similar to itself and blacks out the dissimilar. It creates an attitude that corresponds to it. This automatic phenomenon is an essential cause of the one-sidedness of conscious *orientation* (q.v.). It would lead to a complete loss of equilibrium if there were no self-regulating, compensatory (v. *Compensation*) function in the psyche to correct the conscious attitude. In this sense, therefore, the duality of attitude is a normal phenomenon, and it plays a disturbing role only when the one-sidedness is excessive.

Attitude in the sense of ordinary *attention* can be a relatively unimportant subsidiary phenomenon, but it can also be a general principle governing the whole psyche. Depending on environmental influences and on the individual's education, general experience of life, and personal convictions, a subjective constellation of contents may be habitually present, continually moulding a certain attitude that may affect the minutest details of his life. Every man who is particularly aware of the seamy side of existence, for instance, will naturally have an attitude that is constantly on the look-out for something unpleasant. This conscious imbalance is compensated by an unconscious expectation of pleasure. Again, an oppressed person has a conscious attitude that always anticipates oppression; he selects this factor from the general run of experience and scents it out everywhere. His unconscious attitude, therefore, aims at power and superiority.

The whole psychology of an individual even in its most fundamental features is oriented in accordance with his habitual attitude. Although the general psychological laws operate in every individual, they cannot be said to be characteristic of a particular individual, since the way they operate varies in accordance with his habitual attitude. The habitual attitude is always a resultant of all the factors that exert a decisive influence on the psyche, such as innate disposition, environmental influences, experience of life, insights and convictions gained through *differentiation* (q.v.), *collective* (q.v.) views, etc. Were it not for the absolutely fundamental importance of attitude, the existence of an individual psychology would be out of the question. But the habitual attitude brings about such great displacements of energy, and so modifies the relations between the individual *functions* (q.v.), that effects are produced which often cast doubt on the validity of general psychological laws. In spite of the fact, for instance, that some measure of sexual activity is held to be indispensable on physiological and psychological grounds, there are individuals who, without loss to themselves, i.e., without pathological effects or any demonstrable restriction of their powers, can, to a very great extent, dispense with it, while in other cases quite insignificant disturbances in this area can have far-reaching consequences. How enormous the individual differences are can be seen most clearly, perhaps, in the question of likes and dislikes. Here practically all rules go by the board. What is there, in the last resort, that has not at some time given man pleasure, and what is there that has not caused him pain? Every instinct, every function can be subordinated to another. The ego instinct or power instinct can make sexuality its servant, or sexuality can exploit the ego. Thinking may overrun everything else, or feeling swallow up thinking and sensation, all depending on the attitude.

At bottom, attitude is an individual phenomenon that eludes scientific investigation. In actual experience, however, certain typical attitudes can be distinguished in so far as certain psychic functions can be distinguished. When a function habitually predominates, a typical attitude is produced. According to the nature of the differentiated function, there will be constellations of contents that create a corresponding attitude. There is thus a typical thinking, feeling, sensation, and intuitive attitude. Besides these purely psychological attitudes, whose number might very well be increased, there are also social attitudes, namely, those on which a collective idea has set its stamp. They are characterized by the various "-isms." These collective attitudes are very important, in some cases even outweighing the importance of the individual attitude.

9. COLLECTIVE. I term *collective* all psychic contents that belong not to one individual but to many, i.e., to a society, a people, or to mankind in general. Such contents are what Lévy-Bruhl[18] calls the *représentations collectives* of primitives, as well as general concepts of justice, the state, religion, science, etc., current among civilized man. It is not only concepts and ways of looking at things, however, that must be termed collective, but also *feelings*. Among primitives, the *représentations collectives* are at the same time collective feelings, as Lévy-Bruhl has shown. Because of this collective feeling-value he calls the *représentations collectives* "mystical," since they

18 *How Natives Think*, pp. 35ff.

88

are not merely intellectual but emotional.[19] Among civilized peoples, too, certain collective ideas—God, justice, fatherland, etc.—are bound up with collective feelings. This collective quality adheres not only to particular psychic elements or contents but to whole *functions* (q.v.). Thus the thinking function as a whole can have a collective quality, when it possesses general validity and accords with the laws of logic. Similarly, the feeling function as a whole can be collective, when it is identical with the general feeling and accords with general expectations, the general moral consciousness, etc. In the same way, sensation and intuition are collective when they are at the same time characteristic of a large group of men. The antithesis of collective is *individual* (q.v.).

10. COMPENSATION means *balancing, adjusting, supplementing*. The concept was introduced into the psychology of the neuroses by Adler.[20] He understands by it the functional balancing of the feeling of inferiority by a compensatory psychological system, comparable to the compensatory development of organs in organ inferiority.[21] He says:

With the breaking away from the maternal organism the struggle with the outer world begins for these inferior organs and organ systems, a struggle which must necessarily break out and declare itself with greater violence than in a normally developed apparatus. . . . Nevertheless, the foetal character supplies at the same time the heightened possibility of compensation and overcompensation, increases the capacity for adaptation to usual and unusual resistance, and ensures the development of new and higher forms, of new and higher achievements.[22]

The neurotic's feeling of inferiority, which according to Adler corresponds aetiologically to an organ inferiority, gives rise to an "auxiliary device,"[23] that is, a compensation, which consists in the setting up of a "guiding fiction" to balance the inferiority. The "guiding fiction" is a psychological system that endeavours to turn an inferiority into a superiority. The sig-

[19] Ibid., pp. 36f.

[20] *The Neurotic Constitution.* References to the theory of compensation, originally inspired by G. Anton, are also to be found in Gross.

[21] *Study of Organ Inferiority and Its Psychical Compensation*, p. 73.

[22] Cf. *The Neurotic Constitution*, p. 7.

[23] Cf. ibid., p. 14. [*Hilfskonstruktion*; see also p. xii.—TRANS.]

nificant thing about this conception is the undeniable and empirically demonstrable existence of a compensating function in the sphere of psychological processes. It corresponds to a similar function in the physiological sphere, namely, the self-regulation of the living organism.

Whereas Adler restricts his concept of compensation to the balancing of inferiority feelings, I conceive it as functional adjustment in general, an inherent self-regulation of the psychic apparatus.[24] In this sense, I regard the activity of the *unconscious* (q.v.) as a balancing of the one-sidedness of the general *attitude* (q.v.) produced by the function of *consciousness* (q.v.). Psychologists often compare consciousness to the eye: we speak of a visual field and a focal point of consciousness. The nature of consciousness is aptly characterized by this simile: only a limited number of contents can be held in the conscious field at the same time, and of these only a few can attain the highest grade of consciousness. The activity of consciousness is *selective*. Selection demands *direction*. But direction requires the *exclusion of everything irrelevant*. This is bound to make the conscious *orientation* (q.v.) one-sided. The contents that are excluded and inhibited by the chosen direction sink into the unconscious, where they form a counter-weight to the conscious orientation. The strengthening of this counterposition keeps pace with the increase of conscious one-sidedness until finally a noticeable tension is produced. This tension inhibits the activity of consciousness to a certain extent, and though at first the inhibition can be broken down by increased conscious effort, in the end the tension becomes so acute that the repressed unconscious contents break through in the form of dreams and spontaneous *images* (q.v.). The more one-sided the conscious attitude, the more antagonistic are the contents arising from the unconscious, so that we may speak of a real opposition between the two. In this case the compensation appears in the form of a counter-function, but this case is extreme. As a rule, the unconscious compensation does not run counter to consciousness, but is rather a balancing or supplementing of the conscious orientation. In dreams, for instance, the unconscious supplies all those contents that are

[24] Jung, *Psychological Types* pars. 449ff.

constellated by the conscious situation but are inhibited by conscious selection, although a knowledge of them would be indispensable for complete adaptation.

Normally, compensation is an unconscious process, i.e., an unconscious regulation of conscious activity. In neurosis the unconscious appears in such stark contrast to the conscious state that compensation is disturbed. The aim of analytical therapy, therefore, is a realization of unconscious contents in order that compensation may be re-established.

11. CONCRETISM. By this I mean a peculiarity of thinking and feeling which is the antithesis of *abstraction* (q.v.). The actual meaning of *concrete* is "grown together." A concretely thought concept is one that has grown together or coalesced with other concepts. Such a concept is not abstract, not segregated, not thought "in itself," but is always alloyed and related to something else. It is not a differentiated concept, but is still embedded in the material transmitted by sense-perception. Concretistic *thinking* (q.v.) operates exclusively with concrete concepts and percepts, and is constantly related to *sensation* (q.v.). Similarly, concretistic *feeling* (q.v.) is never segregated from its sensuous context.

Primitive thinking and feeling are entirely concretistic; they are always related to sensation. The thought of the primitive has no detached independence but clings to material phenomena. It rises at most to the level of *analogy*. Primitive feeling is equally bound to material phenomena. Both of them depend on sensation and are only slightly differentiated from it. Concretism, therefore, is an *archaism* (q.v.). The magical influence of the fetish is not experienced as a subjective state of feeling, but sensed as a magical effect. That is concretistic feeling. The primitive does not experience the idea of divinity as a subjective content; for him the sacred tree is the abode of the god, or even the god himself. That is concretistic thinking. In civilized man, concretistic thinking consists in the inability to conceive of anything except immediately obvious facts transmitted by the senses, or in the inability to discriminate between subjective feeling and the sensed object.

Concretism is a concept which falls under the more general concept of *participation mystique* (q.v.). Just as the latter represents a fusion of the individual with external objects, concretism represents a fusion of thinking and feeling with sensation, so that the object of one is at the same time the object of the other. This fusion prevents any differentiation of thinking and feeling and keeps them both within the sphere of sensation; they remain its servants and can never be developed into pure functions. The result is a predominance of the sensation factor in psychological *orientation* (q.v.). (Concerning the importance of this factor, v. *Sensation*.)

The disadvantage of concretism is the subjection of the functions to sensation. Because sensation is the perception of physiological stimuli, concretism either rivets the function to the sensory sphere or constantly leads back to it. This results in a bondage of the psychological functions to the senses, favouring the influence of sensuous facts at the expense of the psychic independence of the individual. So far as the recognition of facts is concerned this orientation is naturally of value, but not as regards the *interpretation* of facts and their relation to the individual. Concretism sets too high a value on the importance of facts and suppresses the freedom of the individual for the sake of objective data. But since the individual is conditioned not merely by physiological stimuli but by factors which may even be opposed to external realities, concretism results in a *projection* (q.v.) of these inner factors into the objective data and produces an almost superstitious veneration of mere facts, as is precisely the case with the primitive. A good example of concretistic feeling is seen in the excessive importance which Nietzsche attached to diet, and in the materialism of Moleschott ("Man is what he eats"). An example of the superstitious overvaluation of facts would be the hypostatizing of the concept of energy in Ostwald's monism.

12. CONSCIOUSNESS. By consciousness I understand the relation of psychic contents to the *ego* (q.v.), in so far as this relation is perceived as such by the ego.[25] Relations to the ego that are not perceived as such are *unconscious* (q.v.). Consciousness is the function or activity[26] which maintains the

[25] Natorp, *Einleitung in die Psychologie nach kritischer Methode*, p. 11. Cf. also Lipps, *Leitfaden der Psychologie*, p. 3.

[26] Riehl, *Zur Einführung in die Philosophie der Gegenwart*, p. 161. Riehl considers consciousness an "activity" or "process."

relation of psychic contents to the ego. Consciousness is not identical with the *psyche* (v. *Soul*), because the psyche represents the totality of all psychic contents, and these are not necessarily all directly connected with the ego, i.e., related to it in such a way that they take on the quality of consciousness. A great many psychic complexes exist which are not all necessarily connected with the ego.[27]

13. CONSTRUCTIVE. This concept is used by me in an equivalent sense to *synthetic*, almost in fact as an illustration of it. Constructive means "building up." I use *constructive* and *synthetic* to designate a method that is the antithesis of the *reductive* (q.v.).[28] The constructive method is concerned with the elaboration of the products of the unconscious (dreams, fantasies, etc.; v. *Fantasy*). It takes the unconscious product as a symbolic expression (v. *Symbol*) which anticipates a coming phase of psychological development.[29] Maeder actually speaks of a *prospective function* of the *unconscious* (q.v.), which half playfully anticipates future developments.[30] Adler, too, recognizes an anticipatory function of the unconscious.[31] It is certain that the product of the unconscious cannot be regarded as a finished thing, as a sort of end-product, for that would be to deny it any purposive significance. Freud himself allows the dream a teleological role at least as the "guardian of sleep,"[32] though for him its prospective function is essentially restricted to "wishing." The purposive character of unconscious tendencies cannot be contested *a priori* if we are to accept their analogy with other psychological or physiological functions. We conceive the product of the unconscious, therefore, as an expression oriented to a goal or purpose, but characterizing its objective in symbolic language.[33]

[27] Jung, "The Psychology of Dementia Praecox." [See also "A Review of the Complex Theory."—EDITORS.]

[28] Jung, *Two Essays on Analytical Psychology*, pars. 121ff.

[29] For a detailed example of this see my "On the Psychology and Pathology of So-called Occult Phenomena," esp. par. 136.

[30] *The Dream Problem*, p. 30.

[31] *The Neurotic Constitution*.

[32] *The Interpretation of Dreams* (Standard Edition, vol. 4), p. 233.

[33] Silberer (*Problems of Mysticism and Its Symbolism*, pp. 241ff.) expresses himself in a similar way in his formulation of *anagogic* significance.

In accordance with this conception, the constructive method of interpretation is not so much concerned with the primary sources of the unconscious product, with its raw materials, so to speak, as with bringing its symbolism to a general and comprehensible expression. The "free associations" of the subject are considered with respect to their aim and not with respect to their derivation. They are viewed from the angle of future action or inaction; at the same time, their relation to the conscious situation is carefully taken into account, for, according to the *compensation* (q.v.) theory, the activity of the unconscious has an essentially complementary significance for the conscious situation. Since it is a question of an anticipatory *orientation* (q.v.), the actual relation to the object does not loom so large as in the reductive procedure, which is concerned with actual relations to the object in the past. It is more a question of the subjective *attitude* (q.v.), the object being little more than a signpost pointing to the tendencies of the subject. The aim of the constructive method, therefore, is to elicit from the unconscious product a meaning that relates to the subject's future attitude. Since, as a rule, the unconscious can create only symbolic expressions, the constructive method seeks to elucidate the symbolically expressed meaning in such a way as to indicate how the conscious orientation may be corrected, and how the subject may act in harmony with the unconscious.

Thus, just as no psychological method of interpretation relies exclusively on the associative material supplied by the analysand, the constructive method also makes use of comparative material. And just as reductive interpretation employs parallels drawn from biology, physiology, folklore, literature, and other sources, the constructive treatment of an intellectual problem will make use of philosophical parallels, while the treatment of an intuitive problem will depend more on parallels from mythology and the history of religion.

The constructive method is necessarily *individualistic,* since a future collective attitude can develop only through the individual. The reductive method, on the contrary, is *collective* (q.v.), since it leads back from the individual to basic collective attitudes or facts. The constructive method can also be directly applied by the subject to his own material, in which case it is an *intuitive* method, employed to elucidate the general meaning of an unconscious product. This elucidation is the result of an *associative* (as distinct from actively *apperceptive*, q.v.) addition of further material, which so enriches the symbolic product (e.g., a dream) that it eventually attains a degree of clarity sufficient for conscious comprehension. It becomes interwoven with more general associations and is thereby assimilated.

14. DIFFERENTIATION means the development of differences, the separation of parts from a whole. In this work I employ the concept of differentiation chiefly with respect to the psychological *functions* (q.v.). So long as a function is still so fused with one or more other functions—thinking with feeling, feeling with sensation, etc.—that it is unable to operate on its own, it is in an *archaic* (q.v.) condition, i.e., not differentiated, not separated from the whole as a special part and existing by itself. Undifferentiated thinking is incapable of thinking apart from other functions; it is continually mixed up with sensations, feelings, intuitions, just as undifferentiated feeling is mixed up with sensations and fantasies, as for instance in the sexualization (Freud) of feeling and thinking in neurosis. As a rule, the undifferentiated function is also characterized by ambivalence and ambitendency,[34] i.e., every position entails its own negation, and this leads to characteristic inhibitions in the use of the undifferentiated function. Another feature is the fusing together of its separate components; thus, undifferentiated sensation is vitiated by the coalescence of different sensory spheres (colour-hearing), and undifferentiated feeling by confounding hate with love. To the extent that a function is largely or wholly unconscious, it is also undifferentiated; it is not only fused together in its parts but also merged with other functions. Differentiation consists in the separation of the function from other functions, and in the separation of its individual parts from each other. Without differentiation direction is impossible, since the direction of a function towards a

---

[34] Bleuler, "Die negative Suggestibilität," *Psychiatrisch-neurologische Wochenschrift*, vol. 6, pp. 249ff.; *The Theory of Schizophrenic Negativism* (orig. in ibid., vol. 12, pp. 171, 189, 195); *Textbook of Psychiatry*, pp. 130, 382. [See also supra, p. 83.—EDITORS.]

goal depends on the elimination of anything irrelevant. Fusion with the irrelevant precludes direction; only a differentiated function is *capable* of being directed.

15. DISSIMILATION, V. ASSIMILATION.

16. EGO. By ego I understand a complex of ideas which constitutes the centre of my field of consciousness and appears to possess a high degree of continuity and identity. Hence I also speak of an *ego-complex*.[35] The ego-complex is as much a content as a condition of *consciousness* (q.v.), for a psychic element is conscious to me only in so far as it is related to my ego-complex. But inasmuch as the ego is only the centre of my field of consciousness, it is not identical with the totality of my psyche, being merely one complex among other complexes. I therefore distinguish between the ego and the *self* (q.v.), since the ego is only the subject of my consciousness, while the self is the subject of my total psyche, which also includes the unconscious. In this sense the self would be an ideal entity which embraces the ego. In unconscious *fantasies* (q.v.) the self often appears as supraordinate or ideal personality, having somewhat the relationship of Faust to Goethe or Zarathustra to Nietzsche. For the sake of idealization the archaic features of the self are represented as being separate from the "higher" self, as for instance Mephistopheles in Goethe, Epimetheus in Spitteler, and in Christian psychology the devil or Antichrist. In Nietzsche, Zarathustra discovered his shadow in the "Ugliest Man."

16a. EMOTION, V. AFFECT.

17. EMPATHY[36] is an *introjection* (q.v.) of the object. For a fuller description of the concept of empathy, see Chapter VII; also *projection*.

18. ENANTIODROMIA means a "running counter to." In the philosophy of Heraclitus[37] it is used to designate the play of

[35] "The Psychology of Dementia Praecox," *Psychiatric Studies*, index, s.v., "ego-complex."

[36] [This appeared as Def. 21, FEELING-INTO, in the Baynes translation.—EDITORS.]

[37] Stobaeus, *Eclogae physicae*, 1, 60: εἱμαρμένην δὲ λόγον ἐκ τῆς ἐναντιοδρομίας δημιουργὸν τῶν ὄντων. ("Fate is the logical product of enantiodromia, creator of all things.")

opposites in the course of events—the view that everything
that exists turns into its opposite. "From the living comes death
and from the dead life, from the young old age and from the
old youth; from waking, sleep, and from sleep, waking; the
stream of generation and decay never stands still."[38] "Construction and destruction, destruction and construction—this is the
principle which governs all the cycles of natural life, from the
smallest to the greatest. Just as the cosmos itself arose from the
primal fire, so must it return once more into the same—a dual
process running its measured course through vast periods of
time, a drama eternally re-enacted."[39] Such is the enantiodromia of Heraclitus in the words of qualified interpreters. He
himself says:

It is the opposite which is good for us.

Men do not know how what is at variance agrees with itself. It is
an attunement of opposite tensions, like that of the bow and the lyre.

The bow ($\beta\iota\acute{o}\varsigma$) is called life ($\beta\acute{\iota}o\varsigma$), but its work is death.

Mortals are immortals and immortals are mortals, the one living
the others' death and dying the others' life.

For souls it is death to become water, for water death to become
earth. But from earth comes water, and from water, soul.

All things are an exchange for fire, and fire for all things, like
goods for gold and gold for goods.

The way up and the way down are the same.[40]

I use the term enantiodromia for the emergence of the
unconscious opposite in the course of time. This characteristic
phenomenon practically always occurs when an extreme, one-
sided tendency dominates conscious life; in time an equally
powerful counterposition is built up, which first inhibits the
conscious performance and subsequently breaks through the
conscious control. Good examples of enantiodromia are: the
conversion of St. Paul and of Raymund Lully,[41] the self-identifi-

[38] Zeller, *A History of Greek Philosophy*, II, p. 17.

[39] Cf. Gomperz, *Greek Thinkers*, I, p. 64.

[40] Cf. Burnet, *Early Greek Philosophy*, pp. 133ff., Fragments 46, 45, 66, 67, 68, 22, 69.

[41] [Ramon Llull, 1234–1315. Cf. "The Psychology of Dementia Praecox," par. 89.—EDITORS.]

cation of the sick Nietzsche with Christ, and his deification and subsequent hatred of Wagner, the transformation of Swedenborg from an erudite scholar into a seer, and so on.

19. EXTRAVERSION is an outward-turning of *libido* (q.v.). I use this concept to denote a manifest relation of subject to object, a positive movement of subjective interest towards the object. Everyone in the extraverted state thinks, feels, and acts in relation to the object, and moreover in a direct and clearly observable fashion, so that no doubt can remain about his positive dependence on the object. In a sense, therefore, extraversion is a transfer of interest from subject to object. If it is an extraversion of thinking, the subject thinks himself into the object; if an extraversion of feeling, he feels himself into it. In extraversion there is a strong, if not exclusive, determination by the object. Extraversion is *active* when it is intentional, and *passive* when the object compels it, i.e., when the object attracts the subject's interest of its own accord, even against his will. When extraversion is habitual, we speak of the extraverted *type* (q.v.).

20. FANTASY.[42] By fantasy I understand two different things: 1. a *fantasm*, and 2. *imaginative activity*. In the present work the context always shows which of these meanings is intended. By fantasy in the sense of *fantasm* I mean a complex of ideas that is distinguished from other such complexes by the fact that it has no objective referent. Although it may originally be based on memory-images of actual experiences, its content refers to no external reality; it is merely the output of creative psychic activity, a manifestation or product of a combination of energized psychic elements. In so far as psychic energy can be voluntarily directed, a fantasy can be consciously and intentionally produced, either as a whole or at least in part. In the former case it is nothing but a combination of *conscious* elements, an artificial experiment of purely theoretical interest. In actual everyday psychological experience, fantasy is either set in motion by an intuitive attitude of expectation, or it is an irruption of *unconscious* contents into consciousness.

[42] [This appeared as Def. 41, PHANTASY, in the Baynes translation.—EDITORS.]

We can distinguish between *active* and *passive* fantasy. *Active* fantasies are the product of *intuition* (q.v.), i.e., they are evoked by an *attitude* (q.v.) directed to the perception of unconscious contents, as a result of which the *libido* (q.v.) immediately invests all the elements emerging from the unconscious and, by association with parallel material, brings them into clear focus in visual form. *Passive* fantasies appear in visual form at the outset, neither preceded nor accompanied by intuitive expectation, the attitude of the subject being wholly passive. Such fantasies belong to the category of psychic *automatisms* (Janet). Naturally, they can appear only as a result of a relative dissociation of the psyche, since they presuppose a withdrawal of energy from conscious control and a corresponding activation of unconscious material. Thus the vision of St. Paul[43] presupposes that unconsciously he was already a Christian, though this fact had escaped his conscious insight.

It is probable that passive fantasies always have their origin in an unconscious process that is antithetical to consciousness, but invested with approximately the same amount of energy as the conscious attitude, and therefore capable of breaking through the latter's resistance. Active fantasies, on the other hand, owe their existence not so much to this unconscious process as to a conscious propensity to assimilate hints or fragments of lightly-toned unconscious complexes and, by associating them with parallel elements, to elaborate them in clearly visual form. It is not necessarily a question of a dissociated psychic state, but rather of a positive participation of consciousness.

Whereas passive fantasy not infrequently bears a morbid stamp or at least shows some trace of abnormality, active fantasy is one of the highest forms of psychic activity. For here the conscious and the unconscious personality of the subject flow together into a common product in which both are united. Such a fantasy can be the highest expression of the unity of a man's *individuality* (q.v.), and it may even create that individuality by giving perfect expression to its unity. As a general rule, passive fantasy is never the expression of a unified indi-

[43] Acts 9:3ff.

99

viduality since, as already observed, it presupposes a considerable degree of dissociation based in turn on a marked conscious/unconscious opposition. Hence the fantasy that irrupts into consciousness from such a state can never be the perfect expression of a unified individuality, but will represent mainly the standpoint of the unconscious personality. The life of St. Paul affords a good example of this: his conversion to Christianity signified an acceptance of the hitherto unconscious standpoint and a repression of the hitherto anti-Christian one, which then made itself felt in his hysterical attacks. Passive fantasy, therefore, is always in need of conscious *criticism*, lest it merely reinforce the standpoint of the unconscious opposite. Whereas active fantasy, as the product of a conscious attitude *not* opposed to the unconscious, and of unconscious processes not opposed but merely compensatory to consciousness, does not require criticism so much as *understanding*.

In fantasies as in dreams (which are nothing but passive fantasies), a *manifest* and a *latent* meaning must be distinguished. The manifest meaning is found in the actual "look" of the fantasy image, in the direct statement made by the underlying complex of ideas. Frequently, however, the manifest meaning hardly deserves its name, although it is always far more developed in fantasies than in dreams, probably because the dream-fantasy usually requires very little energy to overcome the feeble resistance of the sleeping consciousness, with the result that tendencies which are only slightly antagonistic and slightly compensatory can also reach the threshold of perception. Waking fantasy, on the other hand, must muster considerable energy to overcome the inhibition imposed by the conscious attitude. For this to take place, the unconscious opposite must be a very important one in order to break through into consciousness. If it consisted merely of vague, elusive hints it would never be able to direct attention (conscious libido) to itself so effectively as to interrupt the continuity of the conscious contents. The unconscious opposite, therefore, has to depend on a very strong inner cohesion, and this expresses itself in an emphatic manifest meaning.

The manifest meaning always has the character of a visual and concrete process which, because of its objective unreality, can never satisfy the conscious demand for understanding.

Hence another meaning of the fantasy, in other words its interpretation or latent meaning, has to be sought. Although the existence of a latent meaning is by no means certain, and although the very possibility of it may be contested, the demand for understanding is a sufficient motive for a thorough-going investigation. This investigation of the latent meaning may be purely causal, inquiring into the psychological origins of the fantasy. It leads on the one hand to the remoter causes of the fantasy in the distant past, and on the other to ferreting out the instinctual forces which, from the energic standpoint, must be responsible for the fantasy activity. As we know, Freud has made intensive use of this method. It is a method of interpretation which I call *reductive* (q.v.). The justification of a reductive view is immediately apparent, and it is equally obvious that this method of interpreting psychological facts suffices for people of a certain temperament, so that no demand for a deeper understanding is made. If somebody shouts for help, this is sufficiently and satisfactorily explained when it is shown that the man is in immediate danger of his life. If a man dreams of a sumptuous feast, and it is shown that he went to bed hungry, this is a sufficient explanation of his dream. Or if a man who represses his sexuality has sexual fantasies like a medieval hermit, this is satisfactorily explained by a reduction to sexual repression.

But if we were to explain Peter's vision[44] by reducing it to the fact that, being "very hungry," he had received an invitation from the unconscious to eat animals that were "unclean," or that the eating of unclean beasts merely signified the fulfilment of a forbidden wish, such an explanation would send us away empty. It would be equally unsatisfactory to reduce Paul's vision to his repressed envy of the role Christ played among his fellow countrymen, which prompted him to identify himself with Christ. Both explanations may contain some glimmering of truth, but they are in no way related to the real psychology of the two apostles, conditioned as this was by the times they lived in. The explanation is too facile. One cannot discuss historical events as though they were problems of physiology or a purely personal *chronique scandaleuse*. That

---

[44] Acts 10:10ff. and 11:4ff.

would be altogether too limited a point of view. We are therefore compelled to broaden very considerably our conception
of the latent meaning of fantasy, first of all in its causal aspect.
The psychology of an individual can never be exhaustively explained from himself alone: a clear recognition is needed of
the way it is also conditioned by historical and environmental
circumstances. His individual psychology is not merely a physiological, biological, or moral problem, it is also a contemporary problem. Again, no psychological fact can ever be exhaustively explained in terms of causality alone; as a living
phenomenon, it is always indissolubly bound up with the continuity of the vital process, so that it is not only something
evolved but also continually evolving and creative.

Anything psychic is Janus-faced—it looks both backwards
and forwards. Because it is evolving, it is also preparing the
future. Were this not so, intentions, aims, plans, calculations,
predictions and premonitions would be psychological impossi-
bilities. If, when a man expresses an opinion, we simply relate
it to an opinion previously expressed by someone else, this
explanation is quite futile, for we wish to know not merely
what prompted him to do so, but what he means by it, what his
aims and intentions are, and what he hopes to achieve. And
when we know that, we are usually satisfied. In everyday life
we instinctively, without thinking, introduce a final standpoint into an explanation; indeed, very often we take the final
standpoint as the decisive one and completely disregard the
strictly causal factor, instinctively recognizing the creative element in everything psychic. If we do this in everyday life, then
a scientific psychology must take this fact into account, and not
rely exclusively on the strictly causal standpoint originally
taken over from natural science, for it has also to consider the
purposive nature of the psyche.

If, then, everyday experience establishes beyond doubt the
final orientation of conscious contents, we have absolutely no
grounds for assuming, in the absence of experience to the contrary, that this is not the case with the contents of the unconscious. My experience gives me no reason at all to dispute this;
on the contrary, cases where the introduction of the final standpoint alone provides a satisfactory explanation are in the majority. If we now look at Paul's vision again, but this time from

the angle of his future mission, and come to the conclusion that Paul, though consciously a persecutor of Christians, had unconsciously adopted the Christian standpoint, and that he was finally brought to avow it by an irruption of the unconscious, because his unconscious personality was constantly striving toward this goal—this seems to me a more adequate explanation of the real significance of the event than a reduction to personal motives, even though these doubtless played their part in some form or other, since the "all-too-human" is never lacking. Similarly, the clear indication given in Acts 10:28 of a purposive interpretation of Peter's vision is far more satisfying than a merely physiological and personal conjecture.

To sum up, we might say that a fantasy needs to be understood both causally and purposively. Causally interpreted, it seems like a *symptom* of a physiological or personal state, the outcome of antecedent events. Purposively interpreted, it seems like a *symbol*, seeking to characterize a definite goal with the help of the material at hand, or trace out a line of future psychological development. Because active fantasy is the chief mark of the artistic mentality, the artist is not just a *reproducer* of appearances but a creator and educator, for his works have the value of symbols that adumbrate lines of future development. Whether the symbols will have a limited or a general social validity depends on the viability of the creative individual. The more abnormal, i.e., the less viable he is, the more limited will be the social validity of the symbols he produces, though their value may be absolute for the individual himself.

One can dispute the existence of the latent meaning of fantasy only if one is of the opinion that natural processes in general are devoid of meaning. Science, however, has extracted the meaning of natural processes in the form of natural laws. These, admittedly, are human hypotheses advanced in explanation of such processes. But, in so far as we have ascertained that the proposed law actually coincides with the objective process, we are also justified in speaking of the meaning of natural occurrences. We are equally justified in speaking of the meaning of fantasies when it can be shown that they conform to law. But the meaning we discover is satisfying, or to put it another way, the demonstrated law deserves its name, only when it adequately reflects the nature of fantasy. Natural processes both conform to law and demonstrate that law. It is a law that one dreams when one sleeps, but that is not a law which demonstrates anything about the nature of the dream; it is a mere condition of the dream. The demonstration of a physiological source of fantasy is likewise a mere condition of its existence, not a law of its nature. The law of fantasy as a psychological phenomenon can only be a psychological law.

This brings us to the second connotation of fantasy, namely *imaginative activity*. Imagination is the reproductive or creative activity of the mind in general. It is not a special faculty, since it can come into play in all the basic forms of psychic activity, whether *thinking, feeling, sensation,* or *intuition* (qq.v.). Fantasy as imaginative activity is, in my view, simply the direct expression of psychic life,[45] of psychic energy which cannot appear in consciousness except in the form of images or contents, just as physical energy cannot manifest itself except as a definite physical state stimulating the sense organs in physical ways. For as every physical state, from the energic standpoint, is a dynamic system, so from the same standpoint a psychic content is a dynamic system manifesting itself in consciousness. We could therefore say that fantasy in the sense of a fantasm is a definite sum of libido that cannot appear in consciousness in any other way than in the form of an image. A fantasm is an *idée-force*. Fantasy as imaginative activity is identical with the flow of psychic energy.

21. FEELING.[46] I count feeling among the four basic psychological *functions* (q.v.). I am unable to support the psychological school that considers feeling a secondary phenomenon

---

[45][Imaginative activity is therefore not to be confused with "active imagination," a psychotherapeutic method developed by Jung himself. Active imagination corresponds to the definitions of *active fantasy* on p. 99. The method of active imagination (though not called by that name) may be found in "The Aims of Psychotherapy," pars. 101–6, "The Transcendent Function," pars. 166ff., "On the Nature of the Psyche," pars. 400–2, and *Two Essays on Analytical Psychology*, pars. 343ff., 366. The term "active imagination" was used for the first time in *The Tavistock Lecture* (delivered in London, 1935), published as *Analytical Psychology: Its Theory and Practice* (1968). The method is described there on pp. 190ff. (*Coll. Works*, vol. 18.) Further descriptions occur in *Mysterium Coniunctionis*, esp. pars. 706, 749–54.—EDITORS.]

[46][This appeared as Def. 20 in the Baynes translation.—EDITORS.]

dependent on "representations" or sensations, but in company with Höffding, Wundt, Lehmann, Külpe, Baldwin, and others, I regard it as an independent function *sui generis*.[47]

Feeling is primarily a process that takes place between the *ego* (q.v.) and a given content, a process, moreover, that imparts to the content a definite *value* in the sense of acceptance or rejection ("like" or "dislike"). The process can also appear isolated, as it were, in the form of a "mood," regardless of the momentary contents of consciousness or momentary sensations. The mood may be causally related to earlier conscious contents, though not necessarily so, since, as psychopathology amply proves, it may equally well arise from unconscious contents. But even a mood, whether it be a general or only a partial feeling, implies a valuation; not of one definite, individual conscious content, but of the whole conscious situation at the moment, and, once again, with special reference to the question of acceptance or rejection.

Feeling, therefore, is an entirely *subjective* process, which may be in every respect independent of external stimuli, though it allies itself with every sensation.[48] Even an "indifferent" sensation possesses a feeling-tone, namely that of indifference, which again expresses some sort of valuation. Hence feeling is a kind of *judgment*, differing from intellectual judgment in that its aim is not to establish conceptual relations but to set up a subjective criterion of acceptance or rejection. Valuation by feeling extends to *every* content of consciousness, of whatever kind it may be. When the intensity of feeling increases, it turns into an *affect* (q.v.), i.e., a feeling-state accompanied by marked physical innervations. Feeling is distinguished from affect by the fact that it produces no perceptible physical innervations, i.e., neither more nor less than an ordinary thinking process.

[47] For the history both of the theory and concept of feeling, see Wundt, *Outlines of Psychology*, pp. 33ff.; Nahlowsky, *Das Gefühlsleben in seinen wesentlichen Erscheinungen*; Ribot, *The Psychology of the Emotions*; Lehmann, *Die Hauptgesetze des menschlichen Gefühlslebens*; Villa, *Contemporary Psychology*, pp. 182ff.

[48] For the distinction between feeling and sensation, see Wundt, *Grundzüge der physiologischen Psychologie*, I, pp. 350ff.

Ordinary, "simple" feeling is *concrete* (q.v.), that is, it is mixed up with other functional elements, more particularly with sensations. In this case we can call it *affective* or, as I have done in this book, *feeling-sensation*, by which I mean an almost inseparable amalgam of feeling and sensation elements. This characteristic amalgamation is found wherever feeling is still an undifferentiated function, and is most evident in the psyche of a neurotic with differentiated thinking. Although feeling is, in itself, an independent function, it can easily become dependent on another function—thinking, for instance; it is then a mere concomitant of thinking, and is not repressed only in so far as it accommodates itself to the thinking processes.

It is important to distinguish *abstract* feeling from ordinary concrete feeling. Just as the abstract concept (v. *Thinking*) abolishes the differences between things it apprehends, abstract feeling rises above the differences of the individual contents it evaluates, and produces a "mood" or feeling-state which embraces the different individual valuations and thereby abolishes them. In the same way that thinking organizes the contents of consciousness under concepts, feeling arranges them according to their value. The more concrete it is, the more subjective and personal is the value conferred upon them; but the more abstract it is, the more universal and objective the value will be. Just as a completely abstract concept no longer coincides with the singularity and discreteness of things, but only with their universality and non-differentiation, so completely abstract feeling no longer coincides with a particular content and its feeling-value, but with the undifferentiated totality of all contents. Feeling, like thinking, is a *rational* (q.v.) function, since values in general are assigned according to the laws of reason, just as concepts in general are formed according to these laws.

Naturally the above definitions do not give the essence of feeling—they only describe it from outside. The intellect proves incapable of formulating the real nature of feeling in conceptual terms, since thinking belongs to a category incommensurable with feeling; in fact, no basic psychological function can ever be completely expressed by another. That being so, it is impossible for an intellectual definition to reproduce the specific character of feeling at all adequately. The mere classification of feelings adds nothing to an understanding of their nature, because even the most exact classification will be able to indicate only the content of feeling which the intellect can apprehend, without grasping its specific nature. Only as many classes of feelings can be discriminated as there are classes of contents that can be intellectually apprehended, but feeling *per se* can never be exhaustively classified because, beyond every possible class of contents accessible to the intellect, there still exist feelings which resist intellectual classification. The very notion of classification is intellectual and therefore incompatible with the nature of feeling. We must therefore be content to indicate the limits of the concept.

The nature of valuation by feeling may be compared with intellectual *apperception* (q.v.) as an *apperception of value*. We can distinguish *active* and *passive* apperception by feeling. Passive feeling allows itself to be attracted or excited by a particular content, which then forces the feelings of the subject to participate. Active feeling is a transfer of value from the subject; it is an intentional valuation of the content in accordance with feeling and not in accordance with the intellect. Hence active feeling is a *directed* function, an act of the *will* (q.v.), as for instance loving as opposed to being in love. The latter would be *undirected*, passive feeling, as these expressions themselves show: the one is an activity, the other a passive state. Undirected feeling is *feeling-intuition*. Strictly speaking, therefore, only active, directed feeling should be termed *rational*, whereas passive feeling is *irrational* (q.v.) in so far as it confers values without the participation or even against the intentions of the subject. When the subject's attitude as a whole is oriented by the feeling function, we speak of a *feeling type* (v. *Type*).

21a. FEELING, A (or FEELINGS). A feeling is the specific content or material of the feeling function, discriminated by *empathy* (q.v.).

22. FUNCTION (v. also INFERIOR FUNCTION). By a psychological function I mean a particular form of psychic activity that remains the same in principle under varying conditions. From the energic standpoint a function is a manifestation of

libido (q.v.), which likewise remains constant in principle, in much the same way as a physical force can be considered a specific form or manifestation of physical energy. I distinguish four basic functions in all, two rational and two irrational (qq.v.): *thinking* and *feeling, sensation* and *intuition* (qq.v.). I can give no *a priori* reason for selecting these four as basic functions, and can only point out that this conception has shaped itself out of many years' experience. I distinguish these functions from one another because they cannot be related or reduced to one another. The principle of thinking, for instance, is absolutely different from the principle of feeling, and so forth. I make a cardinal distinction between these functions and *fantasies* (q.v.), because fantasy is a characteristic form of activity that can manifest itself in all four functions. Volition or *will* (q.v.) seems to me an entirely secondary phenomenon, and so does *attention*.

23. IDEA. In this work the concept "idea" is sometimes used to designate a certain psychological element which is closely connected with what I term *image* (q.v.). The image may be either *personal* or *impersonal* in origin. In the latter case it is *collective* (q.v.) and is also distinguished by mythological qualities. I then term it a *primordial image*. When, on the other hand, it has no mythological character, i.e., is lacking in visual qualities and merely collective, I speak of an *idea*. Accordingly, I use the term idea to express the *meaning* of a primordial image, a meaning that has been abstracted from the *concretism* (q.v.) of the image. In so far as an idea is an *abstraction* (q.v.), it has the appearance of something derived, or developed, from elementary factors, a product of thought. This is the sense in which it is conceived by Wundt[49] and many others.

In so far, however, as an idea is the formulated meaning of a primordial image by which it was represented *symbolically* (v. *Symbol*), its essence is not just something derived or developed, but, psychologically speaking, exists *a priori*, as a given possibility for thought-combinations in general. Hence, in accordance with its essence (but not with its formulation), the idea is a psychological determinant having an *a priori*

---

[49] "Was soll uns Kant nicht sein?," *Philosophische Studien*, VII, p. 13.

existence. In this sense Plato sees the idea as a prototype of things, while Kant defines it as the "archetype [*Urbild*] of all practical employment of reason," a transcendental concept which as such exceeds the bounds of the experienceable,[50] "a rational concept whose object is not to be found in experience."[51] He says:

Although we must say of the transcendental concepts of reason that *they are only ideas*, this is not by any means to be taken as signifying that they are superfluous and void. For even if they cannot determine any object, they may yet, in a fundamental and unobserved fashion, be of service to the understanding as a canon for its extended and consistent employment. The understanding does not thereby obtain more knowledge of any object than it would have by means of its own concepts, but for the acquiring of such knowledge it receives better and more extensive guidance. Further—what we need here no more than mention—concepts of reason may perhaps make a possible transition from the concepts of nature to the practical concepts, and in that way may give support to the moral ideas themselves.[52]

Schopenhauer says:

By Idea, then, I understand every definite and well-established stage in the objectivation of the Will, so far as the Will is a thing-in-itself and therefore without multiplicity, which stages are related to individual things as their eternal forms or prototypes.[53]

For Schopenhauer the idea is a visual thing, for he conceives it entirely in the way I conceive the primordial image. Nevertheless, it remains uncognizable by the individual, revealing itself only to the "pure subject of cognition," which "is beyond all willing and all individuality."[54]

Hegel hypostatizes the idea completely and attributes to it alone real being. It is the "concept, the reality of the concept, and the union of both."[55] It is "eternal generation."[56] Lasswitz

[50] Cf. Kant, *Critique of Pure Reason* (trans. Kemp Smith), p. 319.

[51] *Logik*, I, sec. 1, par. 3 (*Werke*, ed. Cassirer, VIII, p. 400). [Cf. *Psychological Types*, par. 519, n. 11.]

[52] *Critique of Pure Reason*, pp. 319ff.

[53] Cf. *The World as Will and Idea*, I, p. 168.

[54] Ibid., p. 302. See also infra, par. 752.

[55] *Einleitung in die Aesthetik* (*Sämtliche Werke*, XII), Part I, ch. 1, i.

[56] *The Logic of Hegel* (trans. Wallace), p. 356.

regards the idea as the "law showing the direction in which our experience should develop." It is the "most certain and supreme reality."[57] For Cohen, it is the "concept's awareness of itself," the "foundation" of being.[58]

I do not want to pile up evidence for the primary nature of the idea. These quotations should suffice to show that it can be conceived as a fundamental, a priori factor. It derives this quality from its precursor—the primordial, symbolic image. Its secondary nature as something abstract and derived is a result of the rational elaboration to which the primordial image is subjected to fit it for rational use. The primordial image is an autochthonous psychological factor constantly repeating itself at all times and places, and the same might be said of the idea, although, on account of its rational nature, it is much more subject to modification by rational elaboration and formulations corresponding to local conditions and the spirit of the time. Since it is derived from the primordial image, a few philosophers ascribe a transcendent quality to it; this does not really belong to the idea as I conceive it, but rather to the primordial image, about which a timeless quality clings, being an integral component of the human mind everywhere from time immemorial. Its autonomous character is also derived from the primordial image, which is never "made" but is continually present, appearing in perception so spontaneously that it seems to strive for its own realization, being sensed by the mind as an active determinant. Such a view, however, is not general, and is presumably a question of attitude (q.v., also Ch. VII).

The idea is a psychological factor that not only determines thinking but, as a practical idea, also conditions feeling. As a general rule, I use the term idea only when speaking of the determination of thought in a thinking type, or of feeling in a feeling type. On the other hand, it would be terminologically correct to speak of an a priori determination by the primordial image in the case of an undifferentiated function. The dual nature of the idea as something both primary and derived is responsible for the fact that I sometimes use it promiscuously with primordial image. For the introverted attitude the idea is the prime mover; for the extraverted, a product.

[57] Wirklichkeiten: Beiträge zur Weltverständnis, pp. 152, 154.
[58] Logik der reinen Erkenntnis, pp. 14, 18.

24. IDENTIFICATION. By this I mean a psychological process in which the personality is partially or totally *dissimilated* (v. *Assimilation*). Identification is an alienation of the subject from himself for the sake of the object, in which he is, so to speak, disguised. For example, identification with the father means, in practice, adopting all the father's ways of behaving, as though the son were the same as the father and not a separate individuality. Identification differs from *imitation* in that it is an *unconscious* imitation, whereas imitation is a conscious copying. Imitation is an indispensable aid in developing the youthful personality. It is beneficial so long as it does not serve as a mere convenience and hinder the development of ways and means suited to the individual. Similarly, identification can be beneficial so long as the individual cannot go his own way. But when a better possibility presents itself, identification shows its morbid character by becoming just as great a hindrance as it was an unconscious help and support before. It now has a dissociative effect, splitting the individual into two mutually estranged personalities.

Identification does not always apply to persons but also to things (e.g., a movement of some kind, a business, etc.) and to psychological functions. The latter kind is, in fact, particularly important. Identification then leads to the formation of a secondary character, the individual identifying with his best developed function to such an extent that he alienates himself very largely or even entirely from his original character, with the result that his true *individuality* (q.v.) falls into the unconscious. This is nearly always the rule with people who have one highly differentiated function. It is, in fact, a necessary transitional stage on the way to *individuation* (q.v.).

Identification with parents or the closest members of the family is a normal phenomenon in so far as it coincides with the *a priori family identity*. In this case it is better not to speak of *identification* but of *identity* (q.v.), a term that expresses the actual situation. Identification with members of the family differs from identity in that it is not an *a priori* but a secondary phenomenon arising in the following way. As the individual emerges from the original family identity, the process of adaptation and development brings him up against obstacles that cannot easily be mastered. A damming up of *libido* (q.v.) ensues, which seeks a regressive outlet. The regression reactivates the earlier states, among them the state of family identity. Identification with members of the family corresponds to this regressive revival of an identity that had almost been overcome. All identifications with persons come about in this way. Identification always has a purpose, namely, to obtain an advantage, to push aside an obstacle, or to solve a task in the way another individual would.

25. IDENTITY. I use the term *identity* to denote a psychological conformity. It is always an unconscious phenomenon since a conscious conformity would necessarily involve a consciousness of two dissimilar things, and, consequently, a separation of subject and object, in which case the identity would already have been abolished. Psychological identity presupposes that it is unconscious. It is a characteristic of the primitive mentality and the real foundation of *participation mystique* (q.v.), which is nothing but a relic of the original non-differentiation of subject and object, and hence of the primordial unconscious state. It is also a characteristic of the mental state of early infancy, and, finally, of the unconscious of the civilized adult, which, in so far as it has not become a content of consciousness, remains in a permanent state of identity with objects. Identity with the parents provides the basis for subsequent *identification* (q.v.) with them; on it also depends the possibility of *projection* (q.v.) and *introjection* (q.v.).

Identity is primarily an unconscious conformity with objects. It is not an *equation*, but an *a priori likeness* which was never the object of consciousness. Identity is responsible for the naïve assumption that the psychology of one man is like that of another, that the same motives occur everywhere, that what is agreeable to me must obviously be pleasurable for others, that what I find immoral must also be immoral for them, and so on. It is also responsible for the almost universal desire to correct in others what most needs correcting in oneself. Identity, too, forms the basis of suggestion and psychic infection. Identity is particularly evident in pathological cases, for instance in paranoic ideas of reference, where one's own subjective contents are taken for granted in others. But identity also makes possible a consciously *collective* (q.v.), social *attitude* (q.v.), which found its highest expression in the Christian ideal of brotherly love.

26. IMAGE. When I speak of "image" in this book, I do not mean the psychic reflection of an external object, but a concept derived from poetic usage, namely, a figure of fancy or *fantasy-image*, which is related only indirectly to the perception of an external object. This image depends much more on unconscious fantasy activity, and as the product of such activity it appears more or less abruptly in consciousness, somewhat in the manner of a vision or hallucination, but without possessing the morbid traits that are found in a clinical picture. The image has the psychological character of a fantasy idea and never the quasi-real character of an hallucination, i.e., it never takes the place of reality, and can always be distinguished from sensuous reality by the fact that it is an "inner" image. As a rule, it is not a projection in space, although in exceptional cases it can appear in exteriorized form. This mode of manifestation must be termed *archaic* (q.v.) when it is not primarily pathological, though that would not by any means do away with its archaic character. On the primitive level, however, the inner image can easily be projected in space as a vision or an auditory hallucination without being a pathological phenomenon.

Although, as a rule, no reality-value attaches to the image, this can at times actually increase its importance for psychic life, since it then has a greater *psychological* value, representing an inner reality which often far outweighs the importance of external reality. In this case the *orientation* (q.v.) of the individual is concerned less with adaptation to reality than with adaptation to inner demands.

The inner image is a complex structure made up of the most varied material from the most varied sources. It is no conglomerate, however, but a homogeneous product with a meaning of its own. The image is a *condensed expression of the psychic situation as a whole*, and not merely, nor even predominately, of unconscious contents pure and simple. It undoubtedly does express unconscious contents, but not the whole of them, only those that are momentarily constellated. This constellation is the result of the spontaneous activity of the unconscious on the one hand and of the momentary conscious situation on the other, which always stimulates the activity of relevant subliminal material and at the same time inhibits the irrelevant. Accordingly the image is an expression of the unconscious as well as the conscious situation of the moment. The interpretation of its meaning, therefore, can start neither from the conscious alone nor from the unconscious alone, but only from their reciprocal relationship.

I call the image *primordial* when it possesses an *archaic* (q.v.) character.[60] I speak of its archaic character when the image is in striking accord with familiar mythological motifs. It then expresses material primarily derived from the *collective unconscious* (q.v.), and indicates at the same time that the factors influencing the conscious situation of the moment are *collective* (q.v.) rather than personal. A *personal* image has neither an archaic character nor a collective significance, but expresses contents of the *personal unconscious* (q.v.) and a personally conditioned conscious situation.

The primordial image, elsewhere also termed *archetype*,[61] is always collective, i.e., it is at least common to entire peoples or epochs. In all probability the most important mythological motifs are common to all times and races; I have, in fact, been able to demonstrate a whole series of motifs from Greek mythology in the dreams and fantasies of pure-bred Negroes suffering from mental disorders.[62]

From[63] the scientific, causal standpoint the primordial image can be conceived as a mnemic deposit, an imprint or

[60] A striking example of an archaic image is that of the solar phallus, *Symbols of Transformation*, pars. 151ff.

[61] Jung, "Instinct and the Unconscious," pars. 270ff. See also supra, p. 47.

[62] [In a letter to Freud, Nov. 11, 1912, reporting on a recent visit to the United States, Jung wrote: "I analyzed fifteen Negroes in Washington, with demonstrations." He did this at St. Elizabeths Hospital (a government facility) through the cooperation of its director, Dr. William Alanson White; see *Symbols of Transformation*, par. 154 and n. 52. In late 1912 Jung had already written and partially published *Wandlungen und Symbole der Libido*, and he mentioned the research on Negroes only in its revision, *Symbols of Transformation* (orig. 1952). Cf. also *Analytical Psychology: Its Theory and Practice*, pp. 41ff.—EDITORS.]

[63] [This paragraph has been somewhat revised in *Gesammelte Werke*, vol. 6, and the translation reproduces the revisions.—EDITORS.]

engram (Semon), which has arisen through the condensation of countless processes of a similar kind. In this respect it is a precipitate and, therefore, a typical basic form, of certain ever-recurring psychic experiences. As a mythological motif, it is a continually effective and recurrent expression that reawakens certain psychic experiences or else formulates them in an appropriate way. From this standpoint it is a psychic expression of the physiological and anatomical disposition. If one holds the view that a particular anatomical structure is a product of environmental conditions working on living matter, then the primordial image, in its constant and universal distribution, would be the product of equally constant and universal influences from without, which must, therefore, act like a natural law. One could in this way relate myths to nature, as for instance solar myths to the daily rising and setting of the sun, or to the equally obvious change of the seasons, and this has in fact been done by many mythologists, and still is. But that leaves the question unanswered why the sun and its apparent motions do not appear direct and undisguised as a content of the myths. The fact that the sun or the moon or the meteorological processes appear, at the very least, in allegorized form points to an independent collaboration of the psyche, which in that case cannot be merely a product or stereotype of environmental conditions. For whence would it draw the capacity to adopt a standpoint outside sense perception? How, for that matter, could it be at all capable of any performance more or other than the mere corroboration of the evidence of the senses? In view of such questions Semon's naturalistic and causalistic engram theory no longer suffices. We are forced to assume that the given structure of the brain does not owe its peculiar nature merely to the influence of surrounding conditions, but also and just as much to the peculiar and autonomous quality of living matter, i.e., to a law inherent in life itself. The given constitution of the organism, therefore, is on the one hand a product of external conditions, while on the other it is determined by the intrinsic nature of living matter. Accordingly, the primordial image is related just as much to certain palpable, self-perpetuating, and continually operative natural processes as it is to certain inner determinants of psychic life and of life in general. The organism confronts light with a new structure, the eye, and the psyche confronts the natural process with a symbolic image, which apprehends it in the same way as the eye catches the light. And just as the eye bears witness to the peculiar and spontaneous creative activity of living matter, the primordial image expresses the unique and unconditioned creative power of the psyche.

The primordial image is thus a condensation of the living process. It gives a co-ordinating and coherent meaning both to sensuous and to inner perceptions, which at first appear without order or connection, and in this way frees psychic energy from its bondage to sheer uncomprehended perception. At the same time, it links the energies released by the perception of stimuli to a definite meaning, which then guides action along paths corresponding to this meaning. It releases unavailable, dammed-up energy by leading the mind back to nature and canalizing sheer instinct into mental forms.

The primordial image is the precursor of the *idea* (q.v.), and its matrix. By detaching it from the *concretism* (q.v.) peculiar and necessary to the primordial image, reason develops it into a concept—i.e., an idea which differs from all other concepts in that it is not a datum of experience but is actually the underlying principle of all experience. The idea derives this quality from the primordial image, which, as an expression of the specific structure of the brain, gives every experience a definite form.

The degree of psychological efficacy of the primordial image is determined by the *attitude* (q.v.) of the individual. If the attitude is introverted, the natural consequence of the withdrawal of *libido* (q.v.) from the external object is the heightened significance of the internal object, i.e., thought. This leads to a particularly intense development of thought along the lines unconsciously laid down by the primordial image. In this way the primordial image comes to the surface indirectly. The further development of thought leads to the idea, which is nothing other than the primordial image intellectually formulated. Only the development of the counter-function can take the idea further—that is to say, once the idea has been grasped intellectually, it strives to become effective in life. It therefore calls upon *feeling* (q.v.), which in this case is much less differentiated and more concretistic than thinking.

Feeling is impure and, because undifferentiated, still fused with the *unconscious*. Hence the individual is unable to unite the contaminated feeling with the idea. At this juncture the primordial image appears in the inner field of vision as a *symbol* (q.v.), and, by virtue of its concrete nature, embraces the undifferentiated, concretized feeling, but also, by virtue of its intrinsic significance, embraces the idea, of which it is indeed the matrix, and so unites the two. In this way the primordial image acts as a mediator, once again proving its redeeming power, a power it has always possessed in the various religions. What Schopenhauer says of the idea, therefore, I would apply rather to the primordial image, since, as I have already explained, the idea is not something absolutely *a priori*, but must also be regarded as secondary and derived (v. *Idea*).

In the following passage from Schopenhauer, I would ask the reader to replace the word "idea" by "primordial image," and he will then be able to understand my meaning.

It [the idea] is never cognized by the individual as such, but only by him who has raised himself beyond all willing and all individuality to the pure subject of cognition. Thus it is attainable only by the genius, or by the man who, inspired by works of genius, has succeeded in elevating his powers of pure cognition into a temper akin to genius. It is, therefore, not absolutely but only conditionally communicable, since the idea conceived and reproduced in a work of art, for instance, appeals to each man only according to the measure of his own intellectual worth.

The idea is the unity that falls into multiplicity on account of the temporal and spatial form of our intuitive apprehension.

The concept is like an inert receptacle, in which the things one puts into it lie side by side, but from which no more can be taken out than was put in. The idea, on the other hand, develops, in him who has comprehended it, notions which are new in relation to the concept of the same name: it is like a living, self-developing organism endowed with generative power, constantly bringing forth something that was not put into it.[64]

Schopenhauer clearly discerned that the "idea," or the primordial image as I define it, cannot be produced in the same

[64] Cf. *The World as Will and Idea*, I, pp. 302f.

way that a concept or an "idea" in the ordinary sense can (Kant defines an "idea" as a concept "formed from notions").[65] There clings to it an element beyond rational formulation, rather like Schopenhauer's "temper akin to genius," which simply means a state of feeling. One can get to the primordial image from the idea only because the path that led to the idea passes over the summit into the counterfunction, feeling.

The primordial image has one great advantage over the clarity of the idea, and that is its vitality. It is a self-activating organism, "endowed with generative power." The primordial image is an inherited organization of psychic energy, an ingrained system, which not only gives expression to the energic process but facilitates its operation. It shows how the energic process has run its unvarying course from time immemorial, while simultaneously allowing a perpetual repetition of it by means of an apprehension or psychic grasp of situations so that life can continue into the future. It is thus the necessary counterpart of *instinct* (q.v.), which is a purposive mode of action presupposing an equally purposive and meaningful grasp of the momentary situation. This apprehension is guaranteed by the pre-existent primordial image. It represents the practical formula without which the apprehension of a new situation would be impossible.

26a. IMAGO V. SUBJECTIVE LEVEL.

27. INDIVIDUAL. The psychological individual is characterized by a peculiar and in some respects unique psychology. The peculiar nature of the individual psyche appears less in its elements than in its complex formations. The psychological individual, or his *individuality* (q.v.), has an *a priori* unconscious existence, but exists consciously only so far as a consciousness of his peculiar nature is present, i.e., so far as there exists a conscious distinction from other individuals. The psychic individuality is given *a priori* as a correlate of the physical individuality, although, as observed, it is at first unconscious. A conscious process of *differentiation* (q.v.), or *individuation* (q.v.), is needed to bring the individuality to con-

65 *Critique of Pure Reason*, p. 314.

sciousness, i.e., to raise it out of the state of *identity* (q.v.) with the object. The identity of the individuality with the object is synonymous with its unconsciousness. If the individuality is unconscious, there is no psychological individual but merely a collective psychology of consciousness. The unconscious individuality is then projected on the object, and the object, in consequence, possesses too great a value and acts as too powerful a determinant.

28. INDIVIDUALITY. By individuality I mean the peculiarity and singularity of the individual in every psychological respect. Everything that is not *collective* (q.v.) is individual, everything in fact that pertains only to one individual and not to a larger group of individuals. Individuality can hardly be said to pertain to the psychic elements themselves, but only to their peculiar and unique grouping and combination (v. *Individual*).

29. INDIVIDUATION. The concept of individuation plays a large role in our psychology. In general, it is the process by which individual beings are formed and differentiated; in particular, it is the development of the psychological *individual* (q.v.) as a being distinct from the general, collective psychology. Individuation, therefore, is a process of *differentiation* (q.v.), having for its goal the development of the individual personality.

Individuation is a natural necessity inasmuch as its prevention by a levelling down to collective standards is injurious to the vital activity of the individual. Since *individuality* (q.v.) is a prior psychological and physiological datum, it also expresses itself in psychological ways. Any serious check to individuality, therefore, is an artificial stunting. It is obvious that a social group consisting of stunted individuals cannot be a healthy and viable institution; only a society that can preserve its internal cohesion and collective values, while at the same time granting the individual the greatest possible freedom, has any prospect of enduring vitality. As the individual is not just a single, separate being, but by his very existence presupposes a collective relationship, it follows that the process of individuation must lead to more intense and broader collective relationships and not to isolation.

119

Individuation is closely connected with the *transcendent function* (v. *Symbol*, par. 828), since this function creates individual lines of development which could never be reached by keeping to the path prescribed by collective norms.

Under no circumstances can individuation be the sole aim of psychological education. Before it can be taken as a goal, the educational aim of adaptation to the necessary minimum of collective norms must first be attained. If a plant is to unfold its specific nature to the full, it must first be able to grow in the soil in which it is planted.

Individuation is always to some extent opposed to collective norms, since it means separation and differentiation from the general and a building up of the particular—not a particularity that is *sought out*, but one that is already ingrained in the psychic constitution. The opposition to the collective norm, however, is only apparent, since closer examination shows that the individual standpoint is not *antagonistic* to it, but only *differently oriented*. The individual way can never be directly opposed to the collective norm, because the opposite of the collective norm could only be another, but contrary, norm. But the individual way can, by definition, never be a norm. A norm is the product of the totality of individual ways, and its justification and beneficial effect are contingent upon the existence of individual ways that need from time to time to orient to a norm. A norm serves no purpose when it possesses absolute validity. A real conflict with the collective norm arises only when an individual way is raised to a norm, which is the actual aim of extreme individualism. Naturally this aim is pathological and inimical to life. It has, accordingly, nothing to do with individuation, which, though it may strike out on an individual bypath, precisely on that account needs the norm for its *orientation* (q.v.) to society and for the vitally necessary relationship of the individual to society. Individuation, therefore, leads to a natural esteem for the collective norm, but if the orientation is exclusively collective the norm becomes increasingly superfluous and morality goes to pieces. The more a man's life is shaped by the collective norm, the greater is his individual immorality.

Individuation is practically the same as the development of consciousness out of the original state of *identity* (q.v.). It is thus an extension of the sphere of consciousness, an enriching of conscious psychological life.

30. INFERIOR FUNCTION. This term is used to denote the function that lags behind in the process of *differentiation* (q.v.). Experience shows that it is practically impossible, owing to adverse circumstances in general, for anyone to develop all his psychological functions simultaneously. The demands of society compel a man to apply himself first and foremost to the differentiation of the function with which he is best equipped by nature, or which will secure him the greatest social success. Very frequently, indeed as a general rule, a man identifies more or less completely with the most favoured and hence the most developed function. It is this that gives rise to the various psychological *types* (q.v.). As a consequence of this one-sided development, one or more functions are necessarily retarded. These functions may properly be called *inferior* in a psychological but not psychopathological sense, since they are in no way morbid but merely backward as compared with the favoured function.

Although the inferior function may be conscious as a phenomenon, its true significance nevertheless remains unrecognized. It behaves like many repressed or insufficiently appreciated contents, which are partly conscious and partly unconscious, just as, very often, one knows a certain person from his outward appearance but does not know him as he really is. Thus in normal cases the inferior function remains conscious, at least in its effects; but in a neurosis it sinks wholly or in part into the unconscious. For, to the degree that the greater share of *libido* (q.v.) is taken up by the favoured function, the inferior function undergoes a regressive development; it reverts to the *archaic* (q.v.) stage and becomes incompatible with the conscious, favoured function. When a function that should normally be conscious lapses into the unconscious, its specific energy passes into the unconscious too. A function such as feeling possesses the energy with which it is endowed by nature; it is a well-organized living system that cannot under any circumstances be wholly deprived of its energy. So with the inferior function: the energy left to it passes into the unconscious and activates it in an unnatural way, giving rise to *fantasies* (q.v.) on a level with the archaicized function. In order to extricate the inferior function from the unconscious by analysis, the unconscious fantasy formations that have now been activated must be brought to the surface. The conscious realization of these fantasies brings the inferior function to consciousness and makes further development possible.

31. INSTINCT. When I speak of instinct in this work or elsewhere, I mean what is commonly understood by this word, namely, an *impulsion* towards certain activities. The impulsion can come from an inner or outer stimulus which triggers off the mechanism of instinct psychically, or from organic sources which lie outside the sphere of psychic causality. Every psychic phenomenon is instinctive that does not arise from voluntary causation but from dynamic impulsion, irrespective of whether this impulsion comes directly from organic, extrapsychic sources, or from energies that are merely released by voluntary intention—in the latter case with the qualification that the end-result exceeds the effect voluntarily intended. In my view, all psychic processes whose energies are not under conscious control are instinctive. Thus *affects* (q.v.) are as much instinctive processes as they are *feeling* (q.v.) processes. Psychic processes which under ordinary circumstances are functions of the *will* (q.v.), and thus entirely under conscious control, can, in abnormal circumstances, become instinctive processes when supplied with unconscious energy. This phenomenon occurs whenever the sphere of consciousness is restricted by the repression of incompatible contents, or when, as a result of fatigue, intoxication, or morbid cerebral conditions in general, an *abaissement du niveau mental* (Janet) ensues—when, in a word, the most strongly feeling-toned processes are no longer, or not yet, under conscious control. Processes that were once conscious but in time have become *automatized* I would reckon among the automatic processes rather than the instinctive. Nor do they normally behave like instincts, since in normal circumstances they never appear as impulsions. They do so only when supplied with an energy which is foreign to them.

32. INTELLECT. I call *directed thinking* (q.v.) intellect.

33. INTROJECTION. This term was introduced by Avenarius[66] to correspond with *projection* (q.v.). The expulsion of a subjective content into an object, which is what Avenarius meant, is expressed equally well by the term projection, and it would therefore be better to reserve the term projection for this process. Ferenczi has now defined introjection as the opposite of projection, namely as an indrawing of the object into the subjective sphere of interest, while projection is an expulsion of subjective contents into the object. "Whereas the paranoiac expels from his ego emotions which have become disagreeable, the neurotic helps himself to as large a portion of the outer world as his ego can ingest, and makes this an object of unconscious fantasies."[67] The first mechanism is projection, the second introjection. Introjection is a sort of "diluting process," an "expansion of the circle of interest." According to Ferenczi, the process is a normal one.

Psychologically speaking, introjection is a process of *assimilation* (q.v.), while projection is a process of *dissimilation*. Introjection is an assimilation of object to subject, projection a dissimilation of object from subject through the expulsion of a subjective content into the object (v. *Projection, active*). Introjection is a process of *extraversion* (q.v.), since assimilation to the object requires *empathy* (q.v.) and an investment of the object with *libido* (q.v.). A *passive* and an *active* introjection may be distinguished: transference phenomena in the treatment of the neuroses belong to the former category, and, in general, all cases where the object exercises a compelling influence on the subject, while empathy as a process of adaptation belongs to the latter category.

34. INTROVERSION means an inward-turning of *libido* (q.v.), in the sense of a negative relation of subject to object. Interest does not move towards the object but withdraws from it into the subject. Everyone whose attitude is introverted thinks, feels, and acts in a way that clearly demonstrates that the subject is the prime motivating factor and that the object is of

[66] *Der menschliche Weltbegriff*, pp. 25ff.

[67] "Introjection and Transference," *First Contributions to Psychoanalysis*, pp. 47f.

secondary importance. Introversion may be intellectual or emotional, just as it can be characterized by *sensation* or *intuition* (qq.v.). It is *active* when the subject *voluntarily* shuts himself off from the object, *passive* when he is unable to restore to the object the libido streaming back from it. When introversion is habitual, we speak of an *introverted type* (q.v.).

35. INTUITION (L. *intuéri*, 'to look at or into'). I regard intuition as a basic psychological *function* (q.v.). It is the function that mediates perceptions in an *unconscious way*. Everything, whether outer or inner objects or their relationships, can be the focus of this perception. The peculiarity of intuition is that it is neither sense perception, nor feeling, nor intellectual inference, although it may also appear in these forms. In intuition a content presents itself whole and complete, without our being able to explain or discover how this content came into existence. Intuition is a kind of instinctive apprehension, no matter of what contents. Like *sensation* (q.v.), it is an *irrational* (q.v.) function of perception. As with sensation, its contents have the character of being "given," in contrast to the "derived" or "produced" character of *thinking* and *feeling* (qq.v.) contents. Intuitive knowledge possesses an intrinsic certainty and conviction, which enabled Spinoza (and Bergson) to uphold the *scientia intuitiva* as the highest form of knowledge. Intuition shares this quality with *sensation* (q.v.), whose certainty rests on its physical foundation. The certainty of intuition rests equally on a definite state of psychic "alertness" of whose origin the subject is unconscious.

Intuition may be *subjective* or *objective*: the first is a perception of unconscious psychic data originating in the subject, the second is a perception of data dependent on subliminal perceptions of the object and on the feelings and thoughts they evoke. We may also distinguish *concrete* and *abstract* forms of intuition, according to the degree of participation on the part of sensation. Concrete intuition mediates perceptions concerned with the actuality of things, abstract intuition mediates perceptions of ideational connections. Concrete intuition is a reactive process, since it responds directly to the given facts; abstract intuition, like abstract sensation, needs a certain element of direction, an act of the will, or an aim.

Like sensation, intuition is a characteristic of infantile and primitive psychology. It counterbalances the powerful sense impressions of the child and the primitive by mediating perceptions of mythological images, the precursors of *ideas* (q.v.). It stands in a compensatory relationship to sensation and, like it, is the matrix out of which thinking and feeling develop as rational functions. Although intuition is an irrational function, many intuitions can afterwards be broken down into their component elements and their origin thus brought into harmony with the laws of reason.

Everyone whose general *attitude* (q.v.) is oriented by intuition belongs to the intuitive *type* (q.v.).[68] Introverted and extraverted intuitives may be distinguished according to whether intuition is directed inwards, to the inner vision, or outwards, to action and achievement. In abnormal cases intuition is in large measure fused together with the contents of the *collective unconscious* (q.v.) and determined by them, and this may make the intuitive type appear extremely irrational and beyond comprehension.

36. IRRATIONAL. I use this term not as denoting something *contrary* to reason, but something *beyond* reason, something, therefore, not grounded on reason. Elementary facts come into this category; the fact, for example, that the earth has a moon, that chlorine is an element, that water reaches its greatest density at four degrees centigrade, etc. Another irrational fact is *chance*, even though it may be possible to demonstrate a rational causation after the event.[69]

The irrational is an existential factor which, though it may be pushed further and further out of sight by an increasingly elaborate rational explanation, finally makes the explanation so complicated that it passes our powers of comprehension, the limits of rational thought being reached long before the whole of the world could be encompassed by the laws of reason. A

---

[68] The credit for having discovered the existence of this type belongs to Miss M. Moltzer. [Mary Moltzer, daughter of a Netherlands distiller, took up nursing as a personal gesture against alcoholic abuse and moved to Zurich. She studied under Jung, became an analytical psychologist, and was joint translator of his *The Theory of Psychoanalysis* (see vol. 4, p. 83 and par. 458). She attended the international congress of psychoanalysts at Weimar, 1911.—EDITORS.]

[69] Jung, "Synchronicity: An Acausal Connecting Principle."

completely rational explanation of an object that actually exists (not one that is merely posited) is a Utopian ideal. Only an object that is posited can be completely explained on rational grounds, since it does not contain anything beyond what has been posited by rational thinking. Empirical science, too, posits objects that are confined within rational bounds, because by deliberately excluding the accidental it does not consider the actual object as a whole, but only that part of it which has been singled out for rational observation.

In this sense *thinking* is a *directed function*, and so is *feeling* (qq.v.). When these functions are concerned not with a rational choice of objects, or with the qualities and interrelations of objects, but with the perception of accidentals which the actual object never lacks, they at once lose the attribute of directedness and, with it, something of their rational character, because they then accept the accidental. They begin to be irrational. The kind of thinking or feeling that is directed to the perception of accidentals, and is therefore irrational, is either *intuitive* or *sensational*. Both *intuition* and *sensation* (qq.v.) are functions that find fulfilment in the *absolute perception* of the flux of events. Hence, by their very nature, they will react to every possible occurrence and be attuned to the absolutely contingent, and must therefore lack all rational direction. For this reason I call them irrational functions, as opposed to thinking and feeling, which find fulfilment only when they are in complete harmony with the laws of reason.

Although the irrational as such can never become the object of science, it is of the greatest importance for a practical psychology that the irrational factor should be correctly appraised. Practical psychology stirs up many problems that are not susceptible of a rational solution, but can only be settled irrationally, in a way not in accord with the laws of reason. The expectation or exclusive conviction that there must be a rational way of settling every conflict can be an insurmountable obstacle to finding a solution of an irrational nature.

37. LIBIDO. By libido I mean *psychic energy*.[70] Psychic energy is the *intensity* of a psychic process, its *psychological*

---

[70] *Symbols of Transformation*, Part II, chs. II and III, and "On Psychic Energy," pars. 7ff.

value. This does not imply an assignment of value, whether moral, aesthetic, or intellectual; the psychological value is already implicit in its *determining* power, which expresses itself in definite psychic effects. Neither do I understand libido as a psychic *force*, a misconception that has led many critics astray. I do not hypostatize the concept of energy, but use it to denote intensities or values. The question as to whether or not a specific psychic force exists has nothing to do with the concept of libido. I often use "libido" promiscuously with "energy." The justification for calling psychic energy libido is fully gone into in the works cited in the footnote.

38. OBJECTIVE LEVEL. When I speak of interpreting a dream or fantasy on the objective level, I mean that the persons or situations appearing in it are referred to objectively real persons or situations, in contrast to interpretation on the *subjective level* (q.v.), where the persons or situations refer exclusively to subjective factors. Freud's interpretation of dreams is almost entirely on the objective level, since the dream wishes refer to real objects, or to sexual processes which fall within the physiological, extra-psychological sphere.

39. ORIENTATION. I use this term to denote the general principle governing an *attitude* (q.v.). Every attitude is oriented by a certain viewpoint, no matter whether this viewpoint is conscious or not. A power attitude (v. *Power-complex*) is oriented by the power of the *ego* (q.v.) to hold its own against unfavourable influences and conditions. A thinking attitude is oriented by the principle of logic as its supreme law; a sensation attitude is oriented by the sensuous perception of given facts.

40. PARTICIPATION MYSTIQUE is a term derived from Lévy-Bruhl.[71] It denotes a peculiar kind of psychological connection with objects, and consists in the fact that the subject cannot clearly distinguish himself from the object but is bound to it by a direct relationship which amounts to partial *identity* (q.v.). This identity results from an *a priori* oneness of subject and object. *Participation mystique* is a vestige of this primitive condition. It does not apply to the whole subject-object relation-

[71] *How Natives Think.*

ship but only to certain cases where this peculiar tie occurs. It is a phenomenon that is best observed among primitives, though it is found very frequently among civilized peoples, if not with the same incidence and intensity. Among civilized peoples it usually occurs between persons, seldom between a person and a thing. In the first case it is a transference relationship, in which the object (as a rule) obtains a sort of magical —i.e. absolute—influence over the subject. In the second case there is a similar influence on the part of the thing, or else an *identification* (q.v.) with a thing or the idea of a thing.

41. PERSONA, V. SOUL.

42. POWER-COMPLEX. I occasionally use this term to denote the whole complex of ideas and strivings which seek to subordinate all other influences to the *ego* (q.v.), no matter whether these influences have their source in people and objective conditions or in the subject's own impulses, thoughts, and feelings.

43. PROJECTION means the expulsion of a subjective content into an object; it is the opposite of *introjection* (q.v.). Accordingly it is a process of *dissimilation* (v. *Assimilation*), by which a subjective content becomes alienated from the subject and is, so to speak, embodied in the object. The subject gets rid of painful, incompatible contents by projecting them, as also of positive values which, for one reason or another—self-depreciation, for instance—are inaccessible to him. Projection results from the archaic *identity* (q.v.) of subject and object, but is properly so called only when the need to dissolve the identity with the object has already arisen. This need arises when the identity becomes a disturbing factor, i.e., when the absence of the projected content is a hindrance to adaptation and its withdrawal into the subject has become desirable. From this moment the previous partial identity acquires the character of projection. The term projection therefore signifies a state of identity that has become noticeable, an object of criticism, whether it be the self-criticism of the subject or the objective criticism of another.

We may distinguish *passive* and *active* projection. The passive form is the customary form of all pathological and many normal projections; they are not intentional and are purely automatic occurrences. The active form is an essential component of the act of *empathy* (q.v.). Taken as a whole, empathy is a process of introjection, since it brings the object into intimate relation with the subject. In order to establish this relationship, the subject detaches a content—a feeling, for instance—from himself, lodges it in the object, thereby animating it, and in this way draws the object into the sphere of the subject. The active form of projection is, however, also an act of judgment, the aim of which is to separate the subject from the object. Here a subjective judgment is detached from the subject as a valid statement and lodged in the object; by this act the subject distinguishes himself from the object. Projection, accordingly, is a process of *introversion* (q.v.) since, unlike introjection, it does not lead to ingestion and assimilation but to differentiation and separation of subject from object. Hence it plays a prominent role in paranoia, which usually ends in the total isolation of the subject.

43a. PSYCHE, V. SOUL.

44. RATIONAL. The rational is the reasonable, that which accords with reason. I conceive reason as an *attitude* (q.v.) whose principle it is to conform thought, feeling, and action to objective values. Objective values are established by the everyday experience of external facts on the one hand, and of inner, psychological facts on the other. Such experiences, however, could not represent objective "values" if they were "valued" as such by the subject, for that would already amount to an act of reason. The rational attitude which permits us to declare objective values as valid at all is not the work of the individual subject, but the product of human history.

Most objective values—and reason itself—are firmly established complexes of ideas handed down through the ages. Countless generations have laboured at their organization with the same necessity with which the living organism reacts to the average, constantly recurring environmental conditions, confronting them with corresponding functional complexes, as the eye, for instance, perfectly corresponds to the nature of light. One might, therefore, speak of a pre-existent, metaphysical, universal "Reason" were it not that the adapted reaction of the living organism to average environmental influences is the necessary condition of its existence—a thought already expressed by Schopenhauer. Human reason, accordingly, is nothing other than the expression of man's adaptability to average occurrences, which have gradually become deposited in firmly established complexes of ideas that constitute our objective values. Thus the laws of reason are the laws that designate and govern the average, "correct," adapted *attitude* (q.v.). Everything is "rational" that accords with these laws, everything that contravenes them is "irrational" (q.v.).

Thinking and *feeling* (qq.v.) are rational functions in so far as they are decisively influenced by *reflection*. They function most perfectly when they are in the fullest possible accord with the laws of reason. The irrational functions, *sensation* and *intuition* (qq.v.), are those whose aim is pure *perception*; for, as far as possible, they are forced to dispense with the rational (which presupposes the exclusion of everything that is outside reason) in order to attain the most complete perception of the general flux of events.

45. REDUCTIVE means "leading back." I use this term to denote a method of psychological interpretation which regards the unconscious product not as a *symbol* (q.v.) but *semiotically,* as a *sign* or *symptom* of an underlying process. Accordingly, the reductive method traces the unconscious product back to its elements, no matter whether these be reminiscences of events that actually took place, or elementary psychic processes. The reductive method is oriented backwards, in contrast to the *constructive* (q.v.) method, whether in the purely historical sense or in the figurative sense of tracing complex, differentiated factors back to something more general and more elementary. The interpretive methods of both Freud and Adler are reductive, since in both cases there is a reduction to the elementary processes of wishing or striving, which in the last resort are of an infantile or physiological nature. Hence the unconscious product necessarily acquires the character of an inauthentic expression to which the term "symbol" is not properly applicable. Reduction has a disintegrative effect on the real significance of the unconscious product, since this is either traced back to its historical antecedents and thereby

annihilated, or integrated once again with the same elementary process from which it arose.

46. SELF.[72] As an empirical concept, the self designates the whole range of psychic phenomena in man. It expresses the unity of the personality as a whole. But in so far as the total personality, on account of its unconscious component, can be only in part conscious, the concept of the self is, in part, only *potentially* empirical and is to that extent a *postulate*. In other words, it encompasses both the experienceable and the inexperienceable (or the not yet experienced). It has these qualities in common with very many scientific concepts that are more names than ideas. In so far as psychic totality, consisting of both conscious and unconscious contents, is a postulate, it is a *transcendental* concept, for it presupposes the existence of unconscious factors on empirical grounds and thus characterizes an entity that can be described only in part but, for the other part, remains at present unknowable and illimitable.

Just as conscious as well as unconscious phenomena are to be met with in practice, the self as psychic totality also has a conscious as well as an unconscious aspect. Empirically, the self appears in dreams, myths, and fairytales in the figure of the "supraordinate personality" (v. EGO), such as a king, hero, prophet, saviour, etc., or in the form of a totality symbol, such as the circle, square, *quadratura circuli*, cross, etc. When it represents a *complexio oppositorum*, a union of opposites, it can also appear as a united duality, in the form, for instance, of *tao* as the interplay of *yang* and *yin*, or of the hostile brothers, or of the hero and his adversary (arch-enemy, dragon), Faust and Mephistopheles, etc. Empirically, therefore, the self appears as a play of light and shadow, although conceived as a totality and unity in which the opposites are united. Since such a concept is irrepresentable—*tertium non datur*—it is transcendental on this account also. It would, logically consid-

[72][This definition was written for the *Gesammelte Werke* edition. It may be of interest to note that the definition here given of the self as "the whole range of psychic phenomena in man" is almost identical with the definition of the psyche as "the totality of all psychic processes, conscious as well as unconscious" (p. 134). The inference would seem to be that every individual, by virtue of having, or being, a psyche, is potentially the self. It is only a question of "realizing" it. But the realization, if ever achieved, is the work of a lifetime.—EDITORS.]

ered, be a vain speculation were it not for the fact that it designates symbols of unity that are found to occur empirically.

The self is not a philosophical idea, since it does not predicate its own existence, i.e., does not hypostatize itself. From the intellectual point of view it is only a working hypothesis. Its empirical symbols, on the other hand, very often possess a distinct *numinosity*, i.e., an *a priori* emotional value, as in the case of the mandala,[73] "Deus est circulus . . . ,"[74] the Pythagorean tetraktys,[75] the quaternity,[76] etc. It thus proves to be an *archetypal idea* (v. *Idea; Image*), which differs from other ideas of the kind in that it occupies a central position befitting the significance of its content and its numinosity.

47. SENSATION. I regard sensation as one of the basic psychological *functions* (q.v.). Wundt likewise reckons it among the elementary psychic phenomena.[77] Sensation is the psychological function that mediates the perception of a physical stimulus. It is, therefore, identical with perception. Sensation must be strictly distinguished from *feeling* (q.v.), since the latter is an entirely different process, although it may associate itself with sensation as "feeling-tone." Sensation is related not only to external stimuli but to inner ones, i.e., to changes in the internal organic processes.

[73] [Jung, "A Study in the Process of Individuation" and "Concerning Mandala Symbolism."—EDITORS.]

[74] [The full quotation is "Deus est circulus cuius centrum est ubique, circumferentia vero nusquam" (God is a circle whose centre is everywhere and the circumference nowhere); see "A Psychological Approach to the Dogma of the Trinity," par. 229, n. 6. In this form the saying is a variant of one attributed to St. Bonaventure (*Itinerarium mentis in Deum*, 5): "Deus est figura intellectualis cuius centrum . . ." (God is an intelligible sphere whose centre . . .); see *Mysterium Coniunctionis*, par. 41, n. 42. For more documentation see Borges, "Pascal's Sphere."—EDITORS.]

[75] [Concerning the *tetraktys* see *Psychology and Alchemy*, par. 189; "Commentary on The Secret of the Golden Flower," par. 31; *Psychology and Religion: West and East*, pars. 61, 90, 246.—EDITORS.]

[76] [The quaternity figures so largely in Jung's later writings that the reader who is interested in its numerous significations, including that of a symbol of the self, should consult the indexes (s.v. "quaternity," "self") of *Coll. Works*, vols. 9, Parts I and II, 11, 12, 13, 14.—EDITORS.]

[77] For the history of the concept of sensation see Wundt, *Grundzüge der physiologischen Psychologie*, I, pp. 350ff.; Dessoir, *Geschichte der neueren Psychologie*; Villa, *Contemporary Psychology*; Hartmann, *Die moderne Psychologie*.

Primarily, therefore, sensation is *sense perception*—perception mediated by the sense organs and "body-senses" (kinaesthetic, vasomotor sensation, etc.). It is, on the one hand, an element of ideation, since it conveys to the mind the perceptual image of the external object; and on the other hand, it is an element of feeling, since through the perception of bodily changes it gives feeling the character of an *affect* (q.v.). Because sensation conveys bodily changes to consciousness, it is also a representative of physiological impulses. It is not identical with them, being merely a perceptive function.

A distinction must be made between sensuous or *concrete* (q.v.) sensation and *abstract* (q.v.) sensation. The first includes all the above-mentioned forms of sensation, whereas the second is a sensation that is abstracted or separated from the other psychic elements. Concrete sensation never appears in "pure" form, but is always mixed up with ideas, feelings, thoughts. Abstract sensation is a differentiated kind of perception, which might be termed "aesthetic" in so far as, obeying its own principle, it detaches itself from all contamination with the different elements in the perceived object and from all admixtures of thought and feeling, and thus attains a degree of purity beyond the reach of concrete sensation. The concrete sensation of a flower, on the other hand, conveys a perception not only of the flower as such, but also of the stem, leaves, habitat, and so on. It is also instantly mingled with feelings of pleasure or dislike which the sight of the flower evokes, or with simultaneous olfactory perceptions, or with thoughts about its botanical classification, etc. But abstract sensation immediately picks out the most salient sensuous attribute of the flower, its brilliant redness, for instance, and makes this the sole or at least the principal content of consciousness, entirely detached from all other admixtures. Abstract sensation is found chiefly among artists. Like every abstraction, it is a product of functional *differentiation* (q.v.), and there is nothing primitive about it. The primitive form of a function is always concrete, i.e., contaminated (v. *Archaism*; *Concretism*). Concrete sensation is a reactive phenomenon, while abstract sensation, like every abstraction, is always associated with the *will* (q.v.), i.e., with a sense of direction. The will that is directed to abstract sensation is an expression and application of the *aesthetic sensation attitude*.

Sensation is strongly developed in children and primitives, since in both cases it predominates over thinking and feeling, though not necessarily over *intuition* (q.v.). I regard sensation as conscious, and intuition as unconscious, perception. For me sensation and intuition represent a pair of opposites, or two mutually compensating functions, like thinking and feeling. Thinking and feeling as independent functions are developed, both ontogenetically and phylogenetically, from sensation (and equally, of course, from intuition as the necessary counterpart of sensation). A person whose whole *attitude* (q.v.) is oriented by sensation belongs to the *sensation type* (q.v.).

Since sensation is an elementary phenomenon, it is given *a priori*, and, unlike thinking and feeling, is not subject to rational laws. I therefore call it an *irrational* (q.v.) function, although reason contrives to assimilate a great many sensations into a rational context. Normal sensations are proportionate, i.e., they correspond approximately to the intensity of the physical stimulus. Pathological sensations are disproportionate, i.e., either abnormally weak or abnormally strong. In the former case they are inhibited, in the latter exaggerated. The inhibition is due to the predominance of another function; the exaggeration is the result of an abnormal fusion with another function, for instance with undifferentiated thinking or feeling. It ceases as soon as the function with which sensation is fused is differentiated in its own right. The psychology of the neuroses affords instructive examples of this, since we often find a strong *sexualization* (Freud) of other functions, i.e., their fusion with sexual sensations.

48. SOUL. [Psyche, personality, persona, anima.] I have been compelled, in my investigations into the structure of the unconscious, to make a conceptual distinction between *soul* and *psyche*. By psyche I understand the totality of all psychic processes, conscious as well as unconscious. By soul, on the other hand, I understand a clearly demarcated functional complex that can best be described as a "personality." In order to make clear what I mean by this, I must introduce some further

points of view. It is, in particular, the phenomena of somnambulism, double consciousness, split personality, etc., whose investigation we owe primarily to the French school,[78] that have enabled us to accept the possibility of a plurality of personalities in one and the same individual.

[Soul as a functional complex or "personality"]

It is at once evident that such a plurality of personalities can never appear in a normal individual. But, as the above-mentioned phenomena show, the possibility of a dissociation of personality must exist, at least in the germ, within the range of the normal. And, as a matter of fact, any moderately acute psychological observer will be able to demonstrate, without much difficulty, traces of character-splitting in normal individuals. One has only to observe a man rather closely, under varying conditions, to see that a change from one milieu to another brings about a striking alteration of personality, and on each occasion a clearly defined character emerges that is noticeably different from the previous one. "Angel abroad, devil at home" is a formulation of the phenomenon of character-splitting derived from everyday experience. A particular milieu necessitates a particular *attitude* (q.v.). The longer this attitude lasts, and the more often it is required, the more habitual it becomes. Very many people from the educated classes have to move in two totally different milieus—the domestic circle and the world of affairs. These two totally different environments demand two totally different attitudes, which, depending on the degree of the ego's *identification* (q.v.) with the attitude of the moment, produce a duplication of character. In accordance with social conditions and requirements, the social character is oriented on the one hand by the expectations and demands of society, and on the other by the social aims and aspirations of the individual. The domestic character is, as a rule, moulded by emotional demands and an easy-going acquiescence for the sake of comfort and convenience; whence it frequently happens

---

[78] Azam, *Hypnotisme, double conscience, et altérations de la personnalité*; Prince, *The Dissociation of a Personality*; Landmann, *Die Mehrheit geistiger Persönlichkeiten in einem Individuum*; Ribot, *Die Persönlichkeit*; Flournoy, *From India to the Planet Mars*; Jung, "On the Psychology and Pathology of So-called Occult Phenomena."

that men who in public life are extremely energetic, spirited, obstinate, wilful and ruthless appear good-natured, mild, compliant, even weak, when at home and in the bosom of the family. Which is the true character, the real personality? This question is often impossible to answer.

These reflections show that even in normal individuals character-splitting is by no means an impossiblity. We are, therefore, fully justified in treating personality dissociation as a problem of normal psychology. In my view the answer to the above question should be that such a man has no real character at all: he is not *individual* (q.v.) but *collective* (q.v.), the plaything of circumstance and general expectations. Were he individual, he would have the same character despite the variation of attitude. He would not be identical with the attitude of the moment, and he neither would nor could prevent his *individuality* (q.v.) from expressing itself just as clearly in one state as in another. Naturally he is individual, like every living being, but unconsciously so. Because of his more or less complete identification with the attitude of the moment, he deceives others, and often himself, as to his real character. He puts on a *mask*, which he knows is in keeping with his conscious intentions, while it also meets the requirements and fits the opinions of society, first one motive and then the other gaining the upper hand.

[Soul as persona]

This mask, i.e., the *ad hoc* adopted attitude, I have called the *persona*,[79] which was the name for the masks worn by actors in antiquity. The man who identifies with this mask I would call "personal" as opposed to "individual."

The two above-mentioned attitudes represent two collective personalities, which may be summed up quite simply under the name "personae." I have already suggested that the real individuality is different from both. The persona is thus a functional complex that comes into existence for reasons of adaptation or personal convenience, but is by no means identical with the individuality. The persona is exclusively concerned with the relation to objects. The relation of the individ-

[79] *Two Essays on Analytical Psychology*, pars. 243ff.

ual to the object must be sharply distinguished from the relation to the subject. By the "subject" I mean first of all those vague, dim stirrings, feelings, thoughts, and sensations which flow in on us not from any demonstrable continuity of conscious experience of the object, but well up like a disturbing, inhibiting, or at times helpful, influence from the dark inner depths, from the background and underground vaults of consciousness, and constitute, in their totality, our perception of the life of the unconscious. The subject, conceived as the "inner object," *is* the unconscious. Just as there is a relation to the outer object, an outer attitude, there is a relation to the inner object, an inner attitude. It is readily understandable that this inner attitude, by reason of its extremely intimate and inaccessible nature, is far more difficult to discern than the outer attitude, which is immediately perceived by everyone. Nevertheless, it does not seem to me impossible to formulate it as a concept. All those allegedly accidental inhibitions, fancies, moods, vague feelings, and scraps of fantasy that hinder concentration and disturb the peace of mind even of the most normal man, and that are rationalized away as being due to bodily causes and suchlike, usually have their origin, not in the reasons consciously ascribed to them, but in perceptions of unconscious processes. Dreams naturally belong to this class of phenomena, and, as we all know, are often traced back to such external and superficial causes as indigestion, sleeping on one's back, and so forth, in spite of the fact that these explanations can never stand up to searching criticism. The attitude of the individual in these matters is extremely varied. One man will not allow himself to be disturbed in the slightest by his inner processes—he can ignore them completely; another man is just as completely at their mercy—as soon as he wakes up some fantasy or other, or a disagreeable feeling, spoils his mood for the whole day; a vaguely unpleasant sensation puts the idea into his head that he is suffering from a secret disease, a dream fills him with gloomy forebodings, although ordinarily he is not superstitious. Others, again, have only periodic access to these unconscious stirrings, or only to a certain category of them. For one man they may never have reached consciousness at all as anything worth thinking about, for another they are a worrying problem he broods on daily. One man takes them as physiological, another attributes them to the behaviour of his neighbours, another finds in them a religious revelation.

These entirely different ways of dealing with the stirrings of the unconscious are just as habitual as the attitudes to the outer object. The inner attitude, therefore, is correlated with just as definite a functional complex as the outer attitude. People who, it would seem, entirely overlook their inner psychic processes no more lack a typical inner attitude than the people who constantly overlook the outer object and the reality of facts lack a typical outer one. In all the latter cases, which are by no means uncommon, the persona is characterized by a lack of relatedness, at times even a blind inconsiderateness, that yields only to the harshest blows of fate. Not infrequently, it is just these people with a rigid persona who possess an attitude to the unconscious processes which is extremely susceptible and open to influence. Inwardly they are as weak, malleable, and "soft-centered" as they are inflexible and unapproachable outwardly. Their inner attitude, therefore, corresponds to a personality that is diametrically opposed to the outer personality. I know a man, for instance, who blindly and pitilessly destroyed the happiness of those nearest to him, and yet would interrupt important business journeys just to enjoy the beauty of a forest scene glimpsed from the carriage window. Cases of this kind are doubtless familiar to everyone, so I need not give further examples.

[Soul as anima]

We can, therefore, speak of an inner personality with as much justification as, on the grounds of daily experience, we speak of an outer personality. The inner personality is the way one behaves in relation to one's inner psychic processes; it is the inner attitude, the characteristic face, that is turned towards the unconscious. I call the outer attitude, the outward face, the *persona*; the inner attitude, the inward face, I call the *anima*.[80] To the degree that an attitude is habitual, it is a well-

[80][In the German text the word *Anima* is used only twice: here and on the middle of p. 140. Everywhere else the word used is *Seele* (soul). In this translation *anima* is substituted for "soul" when it refers specifically to the feminine component in a man, just as in Def. 49 (SOUL-IMAGE) *animus* is substituted for "soul" when it refers specifically to the

knit functional complex with which the ego can identify itself more or less. Common speech expresses this very graphically: when a man has an habitual attitude to certain situations, an habitual way of doing things, we say he is quite *another man* when doing this or that. This is a practical demonstration of the autonomy of the functional complex represented by the habitual attitude: it is as though another personality had taken possession of the individual, as though "another spirit had got into him." The same autonomy that very often characterizes the outer attitude is also claimed by the inner attitude, the anima. It is one of the most difficult educational feats to change the persona, the outer attitude, and it is just as difficult to change the anima, since its structure is usually quite as well-knit as the persona's. Just as the persona is an entity that often seems to constitute the whole character of a man, and may even accompany him unaltered throughout his entire life, the anima is a clearly defined entity with a character that, very often, is autonomous and immutable. It therefore lends itself very readily to characterization and description.

As to the character of the anima, my experience confirms the rule that it is, by and large, *complementary* to the character of the persona. The anima usually contains all those common human qualities which the conscious attitude lacks. The tyrant tormented by bad dreams, gloomy forebodings, and inner fears is a typical figure. Outwardly ruthless, harsh, and unapproachable, he jumps inwardly at every shadow, is at the mercy of every mood, as though he were the feeblest and most impressionable of men. Thus his anima contains all those fallible human qualities his persona lacks. If the persona is intellectual, the anima will quite certainly be sentimental. The complementary character of the anima also affects the sexual character, as I have proved to myself beyond a doubt. A very feminine woman has a masculine soul, and a very masculine

---

masculine component in a woman. "Soul" is retained only when it refers to the psychic factor common to both sexes. This distinction is not always easy to make, and the reader may prefer to translate *anima/animus* back into "soul" on occasions when this would help to clarify Jung's argument. For a discussion of this question and the problems involved in translating *Seele* see *Psychology and Alchemy*, par. 9 n. 8. See also *Two Essays on Analytical Psychology*, pars. 296ff., for the relations between *anima/animus* and persona.—EDITORS.]

man has a feminine soul. This contrast is due to the fact that a man is not in all things wholly masculine, but also has certain feminine traits. The more masculine his outer attitude is, the more his feminine traits are obliterated: instead, they appear in his unconscious. This explains why it is just those very virile men who are most subject to characteristic weaknesses; their attitude to the unconscious has a womanish weakness and impressionability. Conversely, it is often just the most feminine women who, in their inner lives, display an intractability, an obstinacy, and a wilfulness that are to be found with comparable intensity only in a man's outer attitude. These are masculine traits which, excluded from the womanly outer attitude, have become qualities of her soul.

If, therefore, we speak of the *anima* of a man, we must logically speak of the *animus* of a woman, if we are to give the soul of a woman its right name. Whereas logic and objectivity are usually the predominant features of a man's outer attitude, or are at least regarded as ideals, in the case of a woman it is feeling. But in the soul it is the other way round: inwardly it is the man who feels, and the woman who reflects. Hence a man's greater liability to total despair, while a woman can always find comfort and hope; accordingly a man is more likely to put an end to himself than a woman. However much a victim of social circumstances a woman may be, as a prostitute for instance, a man is no less a victim of impulses from the unconscious, taking the form of alcoholism and other vices.

As to its common human qualities, the character of the anima can be deduced from that of the persona. Everything that should normally be in the outer attitude, but is conspicuously absent, will invariably be found in the inner attitude. This is a fundamental rule which my experience has borne out over and over again. But as regards its individual qualities, nothing can be deduced about them in this way. We can only be certain that when a man is identical with his persona, his individual qualities will be associated with the anima. This association frequently gives rise in dreams to the symbol of psychic pregnancy, a symbol that goes back to the *primordial image* (q.v.) of the hero's birth. The child that is to be born signifies the individuality, which, though present, is not yet conscious. For in the same way as the persona, the instrument of adaptation to the environment, is strongly influenced by environmental conditions, the anima is shaped by the unconscious and its qualities. In a primitive milieu the persona necessarily takes on primitive features, and the anima similarly takes over the *archaic* (q.v.) features of the unconscious as well as its symbolic, prescient character. Hence the "pregnant," "creative" qualities of the inner attitude.

Identity (q.v.) with the persona automatically leads to an unconscious identity with the anima because, when the ego is not differentiated from the persona, it can have no conscious relation to the unconscious processes. Consequently, it *is* these processes, it is identical with them. Anyone who is himself his outward role will infallibly succumb to the inner processes; he will either frustrate his outward role by absolute inner necessity or else reduce it to absurdity, by a process of *enantiodromia* (q.v.). He can no longer keep to his individual way, and his life runs into one deadlock after another. Moreover, the anima is inevitably projected upon a real object, with which he gets into a relation of almost total dependence. Every reaction displayed by this object has an immediate, inwardly enervating effect on the subject. Tragic ties are often formed in this way (v. *Soul-image*).

49. SOUL-IMAGE [Anima /Animus].[81] The soul-image is a specific *image* (q.v.) among those produced by the unconscious. Just as the *persona* (v. *Soul*), or outer attitude, is represented in dreams by images of definite persons who possess the outstanding qualities of the persona in especially marked form, so in a man the soul, i.e., anima, or inner attitude, is represented in the unconscious by definite persons with the corresponding qualities. Such an image is called a "soul-image." Sometimes these images are of quite unknown or mythological figures. With men the anima is usually personified by the unconscious as a woman; with women the animus is personified as a man. In every case where the *individuality* (q.v.) is unconscious, and therefore associated with the soul, the soul-image has the character of the same sex. In all cases where there is an *identity* (q.v.) with the persona, and the soul accordingly is unconscious, the soul-image is transferred to a real person. This

[81] [See n. 80.—EDITORS.]

person is the object of intense love or equally intense hate (or fear). The influence of such a person is immediate and absolutely compelling, because it always provokes an affective response. The *affect* (q.v.) is due to the fact that a real, conscious adaptation to the person representing the soul-image is impossible. Because an objective relationship is non-existent and out of the question, the *libido* (q.v.) gets dammed up and explodes in an outburst of affect. Affects always occur where there is a failure of adaptation. Conscious adaptation to the person representing the soul-image is impossible precisely because the subject is unconscious of the soul. Were he conscious of it, it could be distinguished from the object, whose immediate effects might then be mitigated, since the potency of the object depends on the *projection* (q.v.) of the soul-image.

For a man, a woman is best fitted to be the real bearer of his soul-image, because of the feminine quality of his soul; for a woman it will be a man. Wherever an impassioned, almost magical, relationship exists between the sexes, it is invariably a question of a projected soul-image. Since these relationships are very common, the soul must be unconscious just as frequently—that is, vast numbers of people must be quite unaware of the way they are related to their inner psychic processes. Because this unconsciousness is always coupled with complete identification with the persona, it follows that this identification must be very frequent too. And in actual fact very many people are wholly identified with their outer attitude and therefore have no conscious relation to their inner processes. Conversely, it may also happen that the soul-image is not projected but remains with the subject, and this results in an identification with the soul because the subject is then convinced that the way he relates to his inner processes is his real character. In that event the persona, being unconscious, will be projected on a person of the same sex, thus providing a foundation for many cases of open or latent homosexuality, and of father-transferences in men or mother-transferences in women. In such cases there is always a defective adaptation to external reality and a lack of relatedness, because identification with the soul produces an attitude predominantly oriented to the perception of inner processes, and the object is deprived of its determining power.

If the soul-image is projected, the result is an absolute affective tie to the object. If it is not projected, a relatively un-adapted state develops, which Freud has described as *narcissism*. The projection of the soul-image offers a release from preoccupation with one's inner processes so long as the be-haviour of the object is in harmony with the soul-image. The subject is then in a position to live out his persona and develop it further. The object, however, will scarcely be able to meet the demands of the soul-image indefinitely, although there are many women who, by completely disregarding their own lives, succeed in representing their husband's soul-image for a very long time. The biological feminine instinct assists them in this. A man may unconsciously do the same for his wife, though this will prompt him to deeds which finally exceed his capacities whether for good or evil. Here again the biological masculine instinct is a help.

If the soul-image is not projected, a thoroughly morbid relation to the unconscious gradually develops. The subject is increasingly overwhelmed by unconscious contents, which his inadequate relation to the object makes him powerless to as-similate or put to any kind of use, so that the whole subject-object relation only deteriorates further. Naturally these two attitudes represent the two extremes between which the more normal attitudes lie. In a normal man the soul-image is not dis-tinguished by any particular clarity, purity, or depth, but is apt to be rather blurred. In men with a good-natured and unag-gressive persona, the soul-image has a rather malevolent char-acter. A good literary example of this is the daemonic woman who is the companion of Zeus in Spitteler's *Olympian Spring*. For an idealistic woman, a depraved man is often the bearer of the soul-image; hence the "saviour fantasy" so frequent in such cases. The same thing happens with men, when the prosti-tute is surrounded with the halo of a soul crying for succour.

50. SUBJECTIVE LEVEL. When I speak of interpreting a dream or fantasy on the subjective level, I mean that the per-sons or situations appearing in it refer to subjective factors en-tirely belonging to the subject's own psyche. As we know, the psychic image of an object is never exactly like the object—at most there is a near resemblance. It is the product of sense per-

ception and *apperception* (q.v.), and these are processes that are inherent in the psyche and are merely stimulated by the object. Although the evidence of our senses is found to coincide very largely with the qualities of the object, our apperception is conditioned by unpredictable subjective influences which render a correct knowledge of the object extraordinarily difficult. Moreover, such a complex psychic factor as a man's character offers only a few *points d'appui* for pure sense perception. Knowledge of human character requires *empathy* (q.v.), reflection, *intuition* (q.v.). As a result of these complications, our final judgment is always of very doubtful value, so that the image we form of a human object is, to a very large extent, subjectively conditioned. In practical psychology, therefore, we would do well to make a rigorous distinction between the image or *imago* of a man and his real existence. Because of its extremely subjective origin, the *imago* is frequently more an image of a subjective functional complex than of the object itself. In the analytical treatment of unconscious products it is essential that the *imago* should not be assumed to be identical with the object; it is better to regard it as an image of the subjective relation to the object. That is what is meant by interpretation on the subjective level.

Interpretation of an unconscious product on the subjective level reveals the presence of subjective judgments and tendencies of which the object is made the vehicle. When, therefore, an object-imago appears in an unconscious product, it is not on that account the image of a real object; it is far more likely that we are dealing with a subjective functional complex (v. *Soul*, pars. 798ff.). Interpretation on the subjective level allows us to take a broader psychological view not only of dreams but also of literary works, in which the individual figures then appear as representatives of relatively autonomous functional complexes in the psyche of the author.

51. SYMBOL. The concept of a *symbol* should in my view be strictly distinguished from that of a *sign*. Symbolic and *semiotic* meanings are entirely different things. In his book on symbolism, Ferrero[82] does not speak of symbols in the strict sense, but of signs. For instance, the old custom of handing

[82] *I simboli in rapporto alla storia e filosofia del dicetto.*

over a piece of turf at the sale of a plot of land might be described as "symbolic" in the vulgar sense of the word, but actually it is purely semiotic in character. The piece of turf is a sign, or token, standing for the whole estate. The winged wheel worn by railway officials is not a *symbol* of the railway, but a *sign* that distinguishes the personnel of the railway system. A symbol always presupposes that the chosen expression is the best possible description or formulation of a relatively unknown fact, which is none the less known to exist or is postulated as existing. Thus, when the badge of a railway official is explained as a symbol, it amounts to saying that this man has something to do with an unknown system that cannot be differently or better expressed than by a winged wheel.

Every view which interprets the symbolic expression as an analogue or an abbreviated designation for a *known* thing is *semiotic*. A view which interprets the symbolic expression as the best possible formulation of a relatively *unknown* thing, which for that reason cannot be more clearly or characteristically represented, is *symbolic*. A view which interprets the symbolic expression as an intentional paraphrase or transmogrification of a known thing is *allegoric*. The interpretation of the cross as a symbol of divine love is *semiotic*, because "divine love" describes the fact to be expressed better and more aptly than a cross, which can have many other meanings. On the other hand, an interpretation of the cross is *symbolic* when it puts the cross beyond all conceivable explanations, regarding it as expressing an as yet unknown and incomprehensible fact of a mystical or transcendent, i.e., psychological, nature, which simply finds itself most appropriately represented in the cross.

So long as a symbol is a living thing, it is an expression for something that cannot be characterized in any other or better way. The symbol is alive only so long as it is pregnant with meaning. But once its meaning has been born out of it, once that expression is found which formulates the thing sought, expected, or divined even better than the hitherto accepted symbol, then the symbol is *dead*, i.e., it possesses only an historical significance. We may still go on speaking of it as a symbol, on the tacit assumption that we are speaking of it as it was before the better expression was born out of it. The way in which St.

Paul and the earlier speculative mystics speak of the cross shows that for them it was still a living symbol which expressed the inexpressible in unsurpassable form. For every esoteric interpretation the symbol is dead, because esotericism has already given it (at least ostensibly) a better expression, whereupon it becomes merely a conventional sign for associations that are more completely and better known elsewhere. Only from the exoteric standpoint is the symbol a living thing.

An expression that stands for a known thing remains a mere sign and is never a symbol. It is, therefore, quite impossible to create a living symbol, i.e., one that is pregnant with meaning, from known associations. For what is thus produced never contains more than was put into it. Every psychic product, if it is the best possible expression at the moment for a fact as yet unknown or only relatively known, may be regarded as a symbol, provided that we accept the expression as standing for something that is only divined and not yet clearly conscious. Since every scientific theory contains an hypothesis, and is therefore an anticipatory description of something still essentially unknown, it is a symbol. Furthermore, every psychological expression is a symbol if we assume that it states or signifies something more and other than itself which eludes our present knowledge. This assumption is absolutely tenable wherever a consciousness exists which is attuned to the deeper meaning of things. It is untenable only when this same consciousness has itself devised an expression which states exactly what it is intended to state—a mathematical term, for instance. But for another consciousness this limitation does not exist. It can take the mathematical term as a symbol for an unknown psychic fact which the term was not intended to express but is concealed within it—a fact which is demonstrably not known to the man who devised the semiotic expression and which therefore could not have been the object of any conscious use.

Whether a thing is a symbol or not depends chiefly on the *attitude* (q.v.) of the observing consciousness; for instance, on whether it regards a given fact not merely as such but also as an expression for something unknown. Hence it is quite possible for a man to establish a fact which does not appear in the least symbolic to himself, but is profoundly so to another consciousness. The converse is also true. There are undoubtedly products whose symbolic character does not depend merely on the attitude of the observing consciousness, but manifests itself spontaneously in the symbolic effect they have on the observer. Such products are so constituted that they would lack any kind of meaning were not a symbolic one conceded to them. Taken as a bare fact, a triangle with an eye enclosed in it is so meaningless that it is impossible for the observer to regard it as a merely accidental piece of foolery. Such a figure immediately conjures up a symbolic interpretation. This effect is reinforced by the widespread incidence of the same figure in identical form, or by the particular care·that went into its production, which is an expression of the special value placed upon it.

Symbols that do not work in this way on the observer are either extinct, i.e., have been superseded by a better formulation, or are products whose symbolic nature depends entirely on the attitude of the observing consciousness. The attitude that takes a given phenomenon as symbolic may be called, for short, the *symbolic attitude*. It is only partially justified by the actual behaviour of things; for the rest, it is the outcome of a definite view of the world which *assigns meaning* to events, whether great or small, and attaches to this meaning a greater value than to bare facts. This view of things stands opposed to another view which lays the accent on sheer facts and subordinates meaning to them. For the latter attitude there can be no symbols whatever when the symbolism depends exclusively on the mode of observation. But even for such an attitude symbols do exist—those, namely, that prompt the observer to conjecture a hidden meaning. A bull-headed god can certainly be explained as a man's body with a bull's head on it. But this explanation can hardly hold its own against the symbolic explanation, because the symbolism is too arresting to be overlooked. A symbol that forcibly obtrudes its symbolic nature on us need not be a *living* symbol. It may have a merely historical or philosophical significance, and simply arouses intellectual or aesthetic interest. A symbol really lives only when it is the best and highest expression for something divined but not yet known to the observer. It then compels his unconscious participation and has a life-giving and life-enhancing effect. As Faust says: "How differently this new sign works upon me!"[83]

[83] [*Goethe's Faust* (trans. MacNeice), p. 22.]

The living symbol formulates an essential unconscious factor, and the more widespread this factor is, the more general is the effect of the symbol, for it touches a corresponding chord in every psyche. Since, for a given epoch, it is the best possible expression for what is still unknown, it must be the product of the most complex and differentiated minds of that age. But in order to have such an effect at all, it must embrace what is common to a large group of men. This can never be what is most differentiated, the highest attainable, for only a very few attain to that or understand it. The common factor must be something that is still so primitive that its ubiquity cannot be doubted. Only when the symbol embraces that and expresses it in the highest possible form is it of general efficacy. Herein lies the potency of the living, social symbol and its redeeming power.

All that I have said about the social symbol applies equally to the individual symbol. There are individual psychic products whose symbolic character is so obvious that they at once compel a symbolic interpretation. For the individual they have the same functional significance that the social symbol has for a larger human group. These products never have an exclusively conscious or an exclusively unconscious source, but arise from the equal collaboration of both. Purely unconscious products are no more convincingly symbolic *per se* than purely conscious ones; it is the symbolic attitude of the observing consciousness that endows them both with the character of a symbol. But they can be conceived equally well as causally determined facts, in much the same way as one might regard the red exanthema of scarlet fever as a "symbol" of the disease. In that case it is perfectly correct to speak of a "symptom" and not of a "symbol." In my view Freud is quite justified when, from his standpoint, he speaks of *symptomatic*[84] rather than symbolic actions, since for him these phenomena are not symbolic in the sense here defined, but are symptomatic signs of a definite and generally known underlying process. There are, of course, neurotics who regard their unconscious products, which are mostly morbid symptoms, as symbols of supreme importance. Generally, however, this is not what happens. On the contrary,

[84] *The Psychopathology of Everyday Life.*

the neurotic of today is only too prone to regard a product that may actually be full of significance as a mere "symptom."

The fact that there are two distinct and mutually contradictory views eagerly advocated on either side concerning the meaning or meaninglessness of things shows that processes obviously exist which express no particular meaning, being in fact mere consequences, or symptoms; and that there are other processes which bear within them a hidden meaning, processes which are not merely derived from something but which seek to become something, and are therefore symbols. It is left to our discretion and our critical judgment to decide whether the thing we are dealing with is a symptom or a symbol.

The symbol is always a product of an extremely complex nature, since data from every psychic function have gone into its making. It is, therefore, neither *rational* nor *irrational* (qq.v.). It certainly has a side that accords with reason, but it has another side that does not; for it is composed not only of rational but also of irrational data supplied by pure inner and outer perception. The profundity and pregnant significance of the symbol appeal just as strongly to *thinking* as to *feeling* (qq.v.), while its peculiar plastic imagery, when shaped into sensuous form, stimulates *sensation* as much as *intuition* (qq.v.). The living symbol cannot come to birth in a dull or poorly developed mind, for such a mind will be content with the already existing symbols offered by established tradition. Only the passionate yearning of a highly developed mind, for which the traditional symbol is no longer the unified expression of the rational and the irrational, of the highest and the lowest, can create a new symbol.

But precisely because the new symbol is born of man's highest spiritual aspirations and must at the same time spring from the deepest roots of his being, it cannot be a onesided product of the most highly differentiated mental functions but must derive equally from the lowest and most primitive levels of the psyche. For this collaboration of opposing states to be possible at all, they must first face one another in the fullest conscious opposition. This necessarily entails a violent disunion with oneself, to the point where thesis and antithesis negate one another, while the ego is forced to acknowledge its absolute participation in both. If there is a subordination of one

149

part, the symbol will be predominantly the product of the other part, and, to that extent, less a symbol than a symptom— a symptom of the suppressed antithesis. To the extent, however, that a symbol is merely a symptom, it also lacks a redeeming effect, since it fails to express the full right of all parts of the psyche to exist, being a constant reminder of the suppressed antithesis even though consciousness may not take this fact into account. But when there is full parity of the opposites, attested by the ego's absolute participation in both, this necessarily leads to a suspension of the *will* (q.v.), for the will can no longer operate when every motive has an equally strong countermotive. Since life cannot tolerate a standstill, a damming up of vital energy results, and this would lead to an insupportable condition did not the tension of opposites produce a new, uniting function that transcends them. This function arises quite naturally from the regression of *libido* (q.v.) caused by the blockage. All progress having been rendered temporarily impossible by the total division of the will, the libido streams backwards, as it were, to its source. In other words, the neutralization and inactivity of consciousness bring about an activity of the unconscious, where all the differentiated functions have their common, archaic root, and where all contents exist in a state of promiscuity of which the primitive mentality still shows numerous vestiges.

From the activity of the unconscious there now emerges a new content, constellated by thesis and antithesis in equal measure and standing in a *compensatory* (q.v.) relation to both. It thus forms the middle ground on which the opposites can be united. If, for instance, we conceive the opposition to be sensuality versus spirituality, then the mediatory content born out of the unconscious provides a welcome means of expression for the spiritual thesis, because of its rich spiritual associations, and also for the sensual antithesis, because of its sensuous imagery. The ego, however, torn between thesis and antithesis, finds in the middle ground its own counterpart, its sole and unique means of expression, and it eagerly seizes on this in order to be delivered from its division. The energy created by the tension of opposites therefore flows into the mediatory product and protects it from the conflict which immediately breaks out again, for both the opposites are striving to get the new product on their side. Spirituality wants to make something spiritual out of it, and sensuality something sensual; the one wants to turn it into science or art, the other into sensual experience. The appropriation or dissolution of the mediatory product by either side is successful only if the ego is not completely divided but inclines more to one side or the other. But if one side succeeds in winning over and dissolving the mediatory product, the ego goes along with it, whereupon an identification of the ego with the most favoured function (v. *Inferior Function*) ensues. Consequently, the process of division will be repeated later on a higher plane.

If, however, as a result of the stability of the ego, neither side succeeds in dissolving the mediatory product, this is sufficient demonstration that it is superior to both. The stability of the ego and the superiority of the mediatory product to both thesis and antithesis are to my mind correlates, each conditioning the other. Sometimes it seems as though the stability of the inborn *individuality* (q.v.) were the decisive factor, sometimes as though the mediatory product possessed a superior power that determines the ego's absolute stability. In reality it may be that the stability of the one and the superior power of the other are two sides of the same coin.

If the mediatory product remains intact, it forms the raw material for a process not of dissolution but of construction, in which thesis and antithesis both play their part. In this way it becomes a new content that governs the whole attitude, putting an end to the division and forcing the energy of the opposites into a common channel. The standstill is overcome and life can flow on with renewed power towards new goals.

I have called this process in its totality the *transcendent function*, "function" being here understood not as a basic function but as a complex function made up of other functions, and "transcendent" not as denoting a metaphysical quality but merely the fact that this function facilitates a transition from one attitude to another. The raw material shaped by thesis and antithesis, and in the shaping of which the opposites are united, is the living symbol. Its profundity of meaning is inherent in the raw material itself, the very stuff of the psyche, transcending time and dissolution; and its configuration by the opposites ensures its sovereign power over all the psychic functions.

Indications of the process of symbol-formation are to be found in the scanty records of the conflicts experienced by the founders of religion during their initiation period, e.g., the struggle between Jesus and Satan, Buddha and Mara, Luther and the devil, Zwingli and his previous worldly life; or the regeneration of Faust through the pact with the devil. In *Zarathustra* we find an excellent example of the suppressed antithesis in the "Ugliest Man."

52. SYNTHETIC, v. CONSTRUCTIVE.

53. THINKING. This I regard as one of the four basic psychological *functions* (q.v.). Thinking is the psychological function which, following its own laws, brings the contents of ideation into conceptual connection with one another. It is an *apperceptive* (q.v.) activity, and as such may be divided into *active* and *passive* thinking. Active thinking is an act of the *will* (q.v.), passive thinking is a mere occurrence. In the former case, I submit the contents of ideation to a voluntary act of judgment; in the latter, conceptual connections establish themselves of their own accord, and judgments are formed that may even contradict my intention. They are not consonant with my aim and therefore, for me, lack any sense of direction, although I may afterwards recognize their directedness through an act of active apperception. Active thinking, accordingly, would correspond to my concept of *directed thinking*.[85] Passive thinking was inadequately described in my previous work as "fantasy thinking."[86] Today I would call it *intuitive* thinking.

To my mind, a mere stringing together of ideas, such as is described by certain psychologists as *associative thinking*,[87] is not thinking at all, but mere ideation. The term "thinking" should, in my view, be confined to the linking up of ideas by means of a concept, in other words, to an act of judgment, no matter whether this act is intentional or not.

The capacity for directed thinking I call *intellect*; the capacity for passive or undirected thinking I call *intellectual intuition*. Further, I call directed thinking a *rational* (q.v.) function, because it arranges the contents of ideation under

[85] *Symbols of Transformation*, pars. 11ff.
[86] Ibid., par. 20.
[87] [Cf. ibid., par. 18, citing James, *The Principles of Psychology*, II, p. 325.]

concepts in accordance with a rational norm of which I am conscious. Undirected thinking is in my view an *irrational* (q.v.) function, because it arranges and judges the contents of ideation by norms of which I am not conscious and therefore cannot recognize as being in accord with reason. Subsequently I may be able to recognize that the intuitive act of judgment accorded with reason, although it came about in a way that appears to me irrational.

Thinking that is governed by *feeling* (q.v.) I do not regard as intuitive thinking, but as a thinking dependent on feeling; it does not follow its own logical principle but is subordinated to the principle of feeling. In such thinking the laws of logic are only ostensibly present; in reality they are suspended in favour of the aims of feeling.

53a. THOUGHT. Thought is the specific content or material of the thinking function, discriminated by *thinking* (q.v.).

54. TRANSCENDENT FUNCTION, V. SYMBOL, p. 149–50.

55. TYPE. A type is a specimen or example which reproduces in a characteristic way the character of a species or class. In the narrower sense used in this particular work, a type is a characteristic specimen of a general *attitude* (q.v.) occurring in many individual forms. From a great number of existing or possible attitudes I have singled out four; those, namely, that are primarily oriented by the four basic psychological *functions* (q.v.): *thinking, feeling, sensation, intuition* (qq.v.). When any of these attitudes is *habitual*, thus setting a definite stamp on the character of an *individual* (q.v.), I speak of a psychological type. These *function-types*, which one can call the thinking, feeling, sensation, and intuitive types, may be divided into two classes according to the quality of the basic function, i.e., into the *rational* and the *irrational* (qq.v.). The thinking and feeling types belong to the former class, the sensation and intuitive types to the latter. A further division into two classes is permitted by the predominant trend of the movement of *libido* (q.v.), namely *introversion* and *extraversion* (qq.v.). All the basic types can belong equally well to one or the other of these classes, according to the predominance of the introverted or

extraverted attitude.[88] A thinking type may belong either to the introverted or to the extraverted class, and the same holds good for the other types. The distinction between rational and irrational types is simply another point of view and has nothing to do with introversion and extraversion.

In my previous contributions to typology[89] I did not differentiate the thinking and feeling types from the introverted and extraverted types, but identified the thinking type with the introverted, and the feeling type with the extraverted. But a more thorough investigation of the material has shown me that we must treat the introverted and extraverted types as categories over and above the function-types. This differentiation, moreover, fully accords with experience, since, for example, there are undoubtedly two kinds of feeling types, the attitude of the one being oriented more by his feeling-experience [= introverted feeling type], the other more by the object [= extraverted feeling type].

56. UNCONSCIOUS. The concept of the *unconscious* is for me an *exclusively psychological* concept, and not a philosophical concept of a metaphysical nature. In my view the unconscious is a psychological borderline concept, which covers all psychic contents or processes that are not conscious, i.e., not related to the *ego* (q.v.) in any perceptible way. My justification for speaking of the existence of unconscious processes at all is derived simply and solely from experience, and in particular from psychopathological experience, where we have undoubted proof that, in a case of hysterical amnesia, for example, the ego knows nothing of the existence of numerous psychic complexes, and the next moment a simple hypnotic procedure is sufficient to bring the lost contents back to memory.

---

[88][Hence the types belonging to the introverted or extraverted class are called *attitude-types*. Cf. supra, p. 1, and *Two Essays on Analytical Psychology*, Part I, ch. IV.—EDITORS.]

[89] "A Contribution to the Study of Psychological Types," infra, Appendix 1; "The Psychology of the Unconscious Processes," *Collected Papers on Analytical Psychology*, pp. 391ff., 401ff.; "The Structure of the Unconscious," *Two Essays on Analytical Psychology*, pars. 462, n. 8, and 482.

Thousands of such experiences justify us in speaking of the existence of unconscious psychic contents. As to the actual state an unconscious content is in when not attached to consciousness, this is something that eludes all possibility of cognition. It is therefore quite pointless to hazard conjectures about it. Conjectures linking up the unconscious state with cerebration and physiological processes belong equally to the realm of fantasy. It is also impossible to specify the range of the unconscious, i.e., what contents it embraces. Only experience can decide such questions.

We know from experience that conscious contents can become unconscious through loss of their energic value. This is the normal process of "forgetting." That these contents do not simply get lost below the threshold of consciousness we know from the experience that occasionally, under suitable conditions, they can emerge from their submersion decades later, for instance in dreams, or under hypnosis, or in the form of cryptomnesia,[90] or through the revival of associations with the forgotten content. We also know that conscious contents can fall below the threshold of consciousness through "intentional forgetting," or what Freud calls the *repression* of a painful content, with no appreciable loss of value. A similar effect is produced by a dissociation of the personality, i.e., the disintegration of consciousness as the result of a violent *affect* (q.v.) or nervous shock, or through the collapse of the personality in schizophrenia (Bleuler).

We know from experience, too, that sense perceptions which, either because of their slight intensity or because of the deflection of attention, do not reach conscious *apperception* (q.v.), none the less become psychic contents through unconscious apperception, which again may be demonstrated by hypnosis, for example. The same thing may happen with certain judgments or other associations which remain unconscious because of their low energy charge or because of the deflection of attention. Finally, experience also teaches that there are unconscious psychic associations—mythological *images* (q.v.), for instance—which have never been the object of con-

[90] Flournoy, *From India to the Planet Mars*; Jung, "On the Psychology and Pathology of So-called Occult Phenomena," pars. 139ff., and "Cryptomnesia."

sciousness and must therefore be wholly the product of unconscious activity.

To this extent, then, experience furnishes *points d'appui* for the assumption of unconscious contents. But it can tell us nothing about what might *possibly* be an unconscious content. It is idle to speculate about this, because the range of what *could* be an unconscious content is simply illimitable. What is the lowest limit of subliminal sense perception? Is there any way of measuring the scope and subtlety of unconscious associations? When is a forgotten content totally obliterated? To these questions there is no answer.

Our experience so far of the nature of unconscious contents permits us, however, to make one general classification. We can distinguish a *personal unconscious*, comprising all the acquisitions of personal life, everything forgotten, repressed, subliminally perceived, thought, felt. But, in addition to these personal unconscious contents, there are other contents which do not originate in personal acquisitions but in the inherited possibility of psychic functioning in general, i.e., in the inherited structure of the brain. These are the mythological associations, the motifs and images that can spring up anew anytime anywhere, independently of historical tradition or migration. I call these contents the *collective unconscious*. Just as conscious contents are engaged in a definite activity, so too are the unconscious contents, as experience confirms. And just as conscious psychic activity creates certain products, so unconscious psychic activity produces dreams, *fantasies* (q.v.), etc. It is idle to speculate on how great a share consciousness has in dreams. A dream presents itself to us: we do not consciously create it. Conscious reproduction, or even the perception of it, certainly alters the dream in many ways, without, however, doing away with the basic fact of the unconscious source of creative activity.

The functional relation of the unconscious processes to consciousness may be described as *compensatory* (q.v.), since experience shows that they bring to the surface the subliminal material that is constellated by the conscious situation, i.e., all those contents which could not be missing from the picture if everything were conscious. The compensatory function of the unconscious becomes more obvious the more one-sided the conscious *attitude* (q.v.) is; pathology furnishes numerous examples of this.

57. WILL. I regard the will as the amount of psychic energy at the disposal of consciousness. Volition would, accordingly, be an energic process that is released by conscious motivation. A psychic process, therefore, that is conditioned by unconscious motivation I would not include under the concept of the will. The will is a psychological phenomenon that owes its existence to culture and moral education, but is largely lacking in the primitive mentality.

EPILOGUE

In our age, which has seen the fruits of the French Revolution—"Liberté, Egalité, Fraternité"—growing into a broad social movement whose aim is not merely to raise or lower political rights to the same general level, but, more hopefully, to abolish unhappiness altogether by means of external regulations and egalitarian reforms—in such an age it is indeed a thankless task to speak of the complete inequality of the elements composing a nation. Although it is certainly a fine thing that every man should stand equal before the law, that every man should have his political vote, and that no man, through hereditary social position and privilege, should have unjust advantage over his brother, it is distinctly less fine when the idea of equality is extended to other walks of life. A man must have a very clouded vision, or view human society from a very misty distance, to cherish the notion that the uniform regulation of life would automatically ensure a uniform distribution of happiness. He must be pretty far gone in delusion if he imagines that equality of income, or equal opportunities for all, would have approximately the same value for everyone. But, if he were a legislator, what would he do about all those people whose greatest opportunities lie not without, but within? If he were just, he would have to give at least twice as much money to the one man as to the other, since to the one it means much, to the other little. No social legislation will ever be able to overcome the psychological differences between men, this most necessary factor for generating the vital energy of a human society. It may serve a useful purpose, therefore, to speak of the heterogeneity of men. These differences involve such different requirements for happiness that no legislation, however perfect, could afford them even approximate satisfaction. No outward form of life could be devised, however equitable and just it might appear, that would not involve injustice for one or the other human type. That, in spite of this, every kind of enthusiast—political, social, philosophical, or religious—is busily en-deavouring to find those uniform external conditions which would bring with them greater opportunities for the happiness of all seems to me connected with a general attitude to life too exclusively oriented by the outer world.

It is not possible to do more than touch on this far-reaching question here, since such considerations lie outside the scope of this book. We are here concerned only with the psycho-logical problem, and the existence of different typical atti-tudes is a problem of the first order, not only for psychology but for all departments of science and life in which man's psychology plays a decisive role. It is, for instance, obvious to anyone of ordinary intelligence that every philosophy that is not just a history of philosophy depends on a personal psycho-logical premise. This premise may be of a purely individual nature, and indeed is generally regarded as such if any psycho-logical criticism is made at all. The matter is then considered settled. But this is to overlook the fact that what one regards as an individual prejudice is by no means so under all circum-stances, since the standpoint of a particular philosopher often has a considerable following. It is acceptable to his followers not because they echo him without thinking, but because it is something they can fully understand and appreciate. Such an understanding would be impossible if the philosopher's stand-point were determined only individually, for it is quite certain in that case that he would be neither fully understood nor even tolerated. The peculiarity of the standpoint which is under-stood and acknowledged by his followers must therefore cor-respond to a *typical* personal attitude, which in the same or a similar form has many representatives in a society. As a rule, the partisans of either side attack each other purely externally, always seeking out the chinks in their opponent's armour. Squabbles of this kind are usually fruitless. It would be of con-siderably greater value if the dispute were transferred to the psychological realm, from which it arose in the first place. The shift of position would soon show a diversity of psychological attitudes, each with its own right to existence, and each con-tributing to the setting up of incompatible theories. So long as one tries to settle the dispute by external compromises, one merely satisfies the modest demands of shallow minds that have never yet been enkindled by the passion of a principle. A real understanding can, in my view, be reached only when the diversity of psychological premises is accepted.

It is a fact, which is constantly and overwhelmingly apparent in my practical work, that people are virtually incapable of understanding and accepting any point of view other than their own. In small things a general superficiality of outlook, combined with a none too common forbearance and tolerance and an equally rare goodwill, may help to build a bridge over the chasm which lack of understanding opens between man and man. But in more important matters, and especially those concerned with ideals, an understanding seems, as a rule, to be beyond the bounds of possibility. Certainly strife and misunderstanding will always be among the props of the tragicomedy of human existence, but it is none the less undeniable that the advance of civilization has led from the law of the jungle to the establishment of courts of justice and standards of right and wrong which are above the contending parties. It is my conviction that a basis for the settlement of conflicting views would be found in the recognition of different types of attitude—a recognition not only of the existence of such types, but also of the fact that every man is so imprisoned in his type that he is simply incapable of fully understanding another standpoint. Failing a recognition of this exacting demand, a violation of the other standpoint is practically inevitable. But just as the contending parties in a court of law refrain from direct violence and submit their claims to the justice of the law and the impartiality of the judge, so each type, conscious of his own partiality, should refrain from heaping abuse, suspicion, and indignity upon his opponent.

In considering the problem of typical attitudes, and in presenting them in outline, I have endeavoured to direct the eye of my readers to this picture of the many possible ways of viewing life, in the hope that I may have contributed my small share to the knowledge of the almost infinite variations and gradations of individual psychology. No one, I trust, will draw the conclusion from my description of types that I believe the four or eight types here presented to be the only ones that exist. This would be a serious misconception, for I have no doubt whatever that these attitudes could also be considered and classified from other points of view. Indeed, there are indications of such possibilities in this book, as for instance Jordan's classification in terms of activity. But whatever the criterion for a classification of types may be, a comparison of the various forms of habitual attitudes will result in an equal number of psychological types.

However easy it may be to regard the existing attitudes from other viewpoints than the one here adopted, it would be difficult to adduce evidence against the existence of psychological types. I have no doubt at all that my opponents will be at some pains to strike the question of types off the scientific agenda, since the type problem must, to say the least of it, be a very unwelcome obstacle for every theory of complex psychic processes that lays claim to general validity. Every theory of complex psychic processes presupposes a uniform human psychology, just as scientific theories in general presuppose that nature is fundamentally one and the same. But in the case of psychology there is the peculiar condition that, in the making of its theories, the psychic process is not merely an object but at the same time the subject. Now if one assumes that the subject is the same in all individual cases, it can also be assumed that the subjective process of theory-making, too, is the same everywhere. That this is not so, however, is demonstrated most impressively by the existence of the most diverse theories about the nature of complex psychic processes. Naturally, every new theory is ready to assume that all other theories were wrong, usually for the sole reason that its author has a different subjective view from his predecessors. He does not realize that the psychology he sees is *his* psychology, and on top of that is the psychology of his type. He therefore supposes that there can be only one true explanation of the psychic process he is investigating, namely the one that agrees with his type. All other views—I might almost say all seven other views —which, in their way, are just as true as his, are for him mere aberrations. In the interests of the validity of his own theory, therefore, he will feel a lively but very understandable distaste for any view that establishes the existence of different types of human psychology, since his own view would then lose, shall we say, seven-eighths of its truth. For, besides his own theory, he would have to regard seven other theories of the same process as equally true, or, if that is saying too much, at least grant a second theory a value equal to his own.

I am quite convinced that a natural process which is very largely independent of human psychology, and can therefore be viewed only as an object, can have but one true explanation. But I am equally convinced that the explanation of a complex psychic process which cannot be objectively registered by any apparatus must necessarily be only the one which that subjective process itself produces. In other words, the author of the concept can produce only just such a concept as corresponds to the psychic process he is endeavouring to explain; but it will correspond only when the process to be explained coincides with the process occurring in the author himself. If neither the process to be explained, nor any analogy of it, were to be found in the author, he would be confronted with a complete enigma, whose explanation he would have to leave to the man who himself experienced the process. If I have a vision, for instance, no objectively registering apparatus will enable me to discover how it originated; I can explain its origin only as I myself understand it. But in this "as I myself understand it" lies the partiality, for at best my explanation will start from the way the visionary process presents itself to me. By what right do I assume that the visionary process presents itself in the same or a similar way to everyone?

With some show of reason, one will adduce the uniformity of human psychology at all times and places as an argument in favour of this generalization of a subjective judgment. I myself am so profoundly convinced of the uniformity of the psyche that I have even summed it up in the concept of the collective unconscious, as a universal and homogeneous substratum whose uniformity is such that one finds the same myth and fairytale motifs in all corners of the earth, with the result that an uneducated American Negro dreams of motifs from Greek mythology[1] and a Swiss clerk re-experiences in his psychosis the vision of an Egyptian Gnostic.[2] But this fundamental homogeneity is offset by an equally great heterogeneity of the

---

1 [*Symbols of Transformation*, par. 154, and supra, par. 747 and n. 62.—EDITORS.]

2 [Vision of the solar phallus. *Symbols of Transformation*, pars. 151ff.; "The Structure of the Psyche," pars. 31ff.; "The Concept of the Collective Unconscious," pars. 104ff.]

conscious psyche. What immeasurable distances lie between the consciousness of a primitive, a Periclean Athenian, and a modern European! What a difference even between the consciousness of a learned professor and that of his spouse! What, in any case, would our world be like if there existed a uniformity of minds? No, the notion of a uniformity of the conscious psyche is an academic chimera, doubtless simplifying the task of a university lecturer when facing his pupils, but collapsing into nothing in the face of reality. Quite apart from the differences among individuals whose innermost natures are separated by stellar distances, the types, as classes of individuals, are themselves to a very large extent different from one another, and it is to the existence of these types that we must ascribe the differences of views in general.

In order to discover the uniformity of the human psyche, I have to descend into the very foundations of consciousness. Only there do I find that in which all are alike. If I build my theory on what is common to all, I explain the psyche in terms of its foundation and origin. But that does nothing to explain its historical and individual differentiation. With such a theory I ignore the peculiarities of the conscious psyche. I actually deny the whole other side of the psyche, its differentiation from the original germinal state. I reduce man to his phylogenetic prototype, or I dissolve him into his elementary processes; and when I try to reconstruct him again, in the former case an ape will emerge, and in the latter a welter of elementary processes engaged in aimless and meaningless reciprocal activity.

No doubt an explanation of the psyche on the basis of its uniformity is not only possible but fully justified. But if I want to project a picture of the psyche in its totality, I must bear in mind the diversity of psyches, since the conscious individual psyche belongs just as much to a general picture of psychology as does its unconscious foundation. In my construction of theories, therefore, I can, with as much right, proceed from the fact of differentiated psyches, and consider the same process from the standpoint of differentiation which I considered before from the standpoint of uniformity. This naturally leads me to a view diametrically opposed to the former one. Everything which in that view was left out of the picture as an individual variant now becomes important as a starting-point for further differentiations; and everything which previously had a special value on account of its uniformity now appears valueless, because merely collective. From this angle I shall always be intent on where a thing is going to, not where it comes from; whereas from the former angle I never bothered about the goal but only about the origin. I can, therefore, explain the same psychic process with two contradictory and mutually exclusive theories, neither of which I can declare to be wrong, since the rightness of one is proved by the uniformity of the psyche, and the rightness of the other by its diversity.

This brings us to the great difficulty which the reading of my earlier book[3] only aggravated, both for the scientific public and for the layman, with the result that many otherwise competent heads were thrown into confusion. There I made an attempt to present both views with the help of case material. But since reality neither consists of theories nor follows them, the two views, which we are bound to think of as divided, are united within it. Each is a product of the past and carries a future meaning, and of neither can it be said with certainty whether it is an end or a beginning. Everything that is alive in the psyche shimmers in rainbow hues. For anyone who thinks there is only one true explanation of a psychic process, this vitality of psychic contents, which necessitates two contradictory theories, is a matter for despair, especially if he is enamoured of simple and uncomplicated truths, incapable maybe of thinking both at the same time.

On the other hand, I am not convinced that, with these two ways of looking at the psyche—the reductive and constructive as I have called them[4]—the possibilities of explanation are exhausted. I believe that other equally "true" explanations of the psychic process can still be put forward, just as many in fact as there are types. Moreover, these explanations will agree as well or as ill with one another as the types themselves in their personal relations. Should, therefore, the existence of typical differences of human psyches be granted—and I confess I see no reason why it should not be granted—the

---

[3] *Symbols of Transformation.*

[4] "On Psychological Understanding," pars. 391ff. [Also *Two Essays on Analytical Psychology*, pars. 121ff.]

scientific theorist is confronted with the disagreeable dilemma of either allowing several contradictory theories of the same process to exist side by side, or of making an attempt, foredoomed at the outset, to found a sect which claims for itself the only correct method and the only true theory. Not only does the former possibility encounter the extraordinary difficulty of an inwardly contradictory "double-think" operation, it also contravenes one of the first principles of intellectual morality: *principia explicandi non sunt multiplicanda praeter necessitatem*.[5] But in the case of psychological theories the necessity of a plurality of explanations is given from the start, since, in contrast to any other scientific theory, the object of psychological explanation is consubstantial with the subject: one psychological process has to explain another. This serious difficulty has already driven thoughtful persons to remarkable subterfuges, such as the assumption of an "objective intellect" standing outside the psychic process and capable of contemplating the subordinate psyche objectively, or the similar assumption that the intellect is a faculty which can stand outside itself and contemplate itself. All these expedients are supposed to create a sort of extra-terrestrial Archimedean point by means of which the intellect can lift itself off its own hinges. I understand very well the profound human need for convenient solutions, but I do not see why truth should bow to this need. I can also understand that, aesthetically, it would be far more satisfactory if, instead of the paradox of mutually contradictory explanations, we could reduce the psychic process to the simplest possible instinctive foundation and leave it at that, or if we could credit it with a metaphysical goal of redemption and find peace in that hope.

Whatever we strive to fathom with our intellect will end in paradox and relativity, if it be honest work and not *a petitio principii* in the interests of convenience. That an intellectual understanding of the psychic process must end in paradox and relativity is simply unavoidable, if only for the reason that the intellect is but one of many psychic functions which is intended by nature to serve man in constructing of his images of the ob-

[5] ["Explanatory principles are not to be multiplied beyond the necessary": Occam's Razor.—TRANSLATOR.]

jective world. We should not pretend to understand the world only by the intellect; we apprehend it just as much by feeling. Therefore the judgment of the intellect is, at best, only a half-truth, and must, if it is honest, also admit its inadequacy.

To deny the existence of types is of little avail in the face of the facts. In view of their existence, therefore, every theory of psychic processes has to submit to being evaluated in its turn as itself a psychic process, as the expression of a specific type of human psychology with its own justification. Only from these typical self-representations of the psyche can the materials be collected which will co-operate to form a higher synthesis.

BIBLIOGRAPHY

ADLER, ALFRED. *The Neurotic Constitution.* Translated by Bernard Glueck and John E. Lind. New York, 1916. (Original: *Über den nervösen Charakter.* Wiesbaden, 1912.)

———. *Study of Organ Inferiority and Its Physical Compensation.* Translated by Smith Ely Jelliffe. (Nervous and Mental Disease Monographs, 24.) New York, 1917. (Original: *Studie über Minderwertigkeit von Organen.* Vienna, 1907.)

AVENARIUS, RICHARD. *Der Menschliche Weltbegriff.* Leipzig, 1891.

AZAM, C. M. ÉTIENNE EUGÈNE. *Hypnotisme, double conscience, et altérations de la personnalité.* Paris, 1887.

BINSWANGER, LUDWIG. "On the Psychogalvanic Phenomena in Association Experiments." In: C. G. JUNG (ed.). *Studies in Word-Association.* Translated by M. D. Eder. London, 1918; New York, 1919.

BLEULER, EUGEN. "Die negative Suggestibilität, ein psychologisches Prototyp des Negativismus," *Psychiatrisch-neurologische Wochenschrift* (Halle), VI (1904), 249–69.

———. "Affectivity, Suggestibility, Paranoia" (translated by Charles Ricksher), *New York State Hospitals Bulletin* (Utica, N.Y.), V (1912), pp. 481ff. (Original: *Affectivität, Suggestibilität, Paranoia.* Halle, 1906.)

———. *Textbook of Psychiatry.* Translated by A. A. Brill. New York and London, 1924. (Original: *Lehrbuch der Psychiatrie.* Berlin, 1916.)

———. *The Theory of Schizophrenic Negativism.* Translated by William A. White. (Nervous and Mental Disease Monograph Series, 11.) New York, 1912. (Original: "Zur Theorie des schizophrenen Negativismus," *Psychiatrisch-neurologische Wochenschrift* (Halle), XII (1910–11), 171, 189, 195.)

BORGES, JORGE LUIS. "Pascal's Sphere." In: *Other Inquisitions.* Translated by Ruth L. C. Simms. Austin, Tex., 1964. (Original: "La esfera de Pascal," in *Otras Inquisiciones.* (Obras Completas, 8.) Buenos Aires, 1960.)

BURNET, JOHN. *Early Greek Philosophy.* 4th edn., London, 1930.

COHEN, HERMANN. *Logik der reinen Erkenntnis.* Berlin, 1902.

DESSOIR, MAX. *Geschichte der neueren deutschen Psychologie.* Vol. I: *Von Leibniz bis Kant.* Berlin, 1894; 2nd edn., 1902.

FÉRÉ, CHARLES. "Note sur des modifications de la résistance électrique sous l'influence des excitations sensorielles et des émotions," *Comptes-rendus hebdomadaires des séances et memoires de la Société de Biologie* (Paris), ser. 8, V (1888), 217–19.

FERENCZI, SANDOR. "Introjection and Transference." In: *First Contributions to Psycho-Analysis.* Translated by Ernest Jones. London, 1952. (Pp. 35–93.) (Original: "Introjecktion und Übertragung," *Jahrbuch für psychoanalytische und psychopathologische Forschungen* (Vienna), II (1910).

FLOURNOY, THÉDORE. *From India to the Planet Mars.* Translated by D. B. Vermilye. New York, 1900. (Original: *Des Indies à la planète Mars.* 3rd edn., Paris, 1900.)

FREUD, SIGMUND. *The Interpretation of Dreams.* (Complete Psychological Works, 4 and 5.) Translated by James Strachey. London, 1953. 2 vols. (Original: *Die Traumdeutung.* 1900.)

——. *The Psychopathology of Everyday Life.* (Complete Psychological Works, 6.) Translated by Alan Tyson. London, 1960. (Original: *Zur Psychopathologie des Alltagsleben.* 1901.)

GOETHE, JOHANN WOLFGANG. *Goethe's Faust.* Parts I and II. An abridged version translated by Louis MacNeice. London and New York, 1952.

GOMPERZ, THEODOR. *Greek Thinkers.* Translated by Laurie Magnus and G. G. Berry. London, 1901–12. 4 vols. (Original: *Griechische Denker.* 3rd edn., Leipzig, 1911–12.)

HARTMANN, EDUARD VON. *Die moderne Psychologie.* (Ausgewählte Werke, 13.) Leipzig, 1901.

HEGEL, GEORG WILHELM FRIEDRICH. *The Logic of Hegel.* Translated by William Wallace. 2nd edn., Oxford, 1892.

——. *Einleitung in die Aesthetik.* (Särtliche Werke, Jubiläumsausgabe, edited by Hermann Glockner, 12.) Stuttgart, 1927.

JACOBI, JOLANDE. *Complex/Archetype/Symbol in the Psychology of C. G. Jung.* Translated by Ralph Manheim. New York (Bollingen Series) and London, 1959.

JAMES, WILLIAM. *The Principles of Psychology.* New York, 1890. 2 vols.

JUNG, CARL GUSTAV.* "The Aims of Psychotherapy." In *Collected Works,* 16.

*For details of *The Collected Works of C. G. Jung,* see list at the end of this volume.

——. *Analytical Psychology: Its Theory and Practice*. New York and London, 1968. (Published as "The Tavistock Lectures" in *Collected Works*, 18.)

——. *Collected Papers on Analytical Psychology*. Edited by Constance E. Long. London and New York, 1916; 2nd edn., 1917.

——. "The Concept of the Collective Unconscious." In *Collected Works*, 9, i.

——. "Concerning Mandala Symbolism." In *Collected Works*, 9, I.

——. "Instinct and the Unconscious." In *Collected Works*, 8.

——. *Mysterium Coniunctionis*. *Collected Works*, 14.

——. "On the Nature of the Psyche." In *Collected Works*, 8.

——. "On Psychic Energy." In *Collected Works*, 8.

——. "On Psychological Understanding." In *Collected Works*, 3.

——. "On the Psychology and Pathology of So-called Occult Phenomena." In *Collected Works*, 1.

——. "On Psychophysical Relations of the Association Experiments." In *Collected Works*, 2.

——. "A Psychological Approach to the Dogma of the Trinity." In *Collected Works*, 11.

——. *Psychology and Alchemy*. *Collected Works*, 12.

——. *Psychology and Religion: West and East*. *Collected Works*, 11.

——. "The Psychology of Dementia Praecox." In *Collected Works*, 3.

——. *Psychology of the Unconscious: A Study of the Transformations and Symbolisms of the Libido*. Translated by Beatrice M. Hinkle. New York, 1916; London, 1917. (Original: *Wandlungen und Symbole der Libido*. Vienna, 1912.) Revised as *Symbols of Transformation*, q.v.

——. "A Review of the Complex Theory." In *Collected Works*, 8.

——. "The Structure of the Psyche." In *Collected Works*, 8.

——. *Studies in Word-Association*. Under the direction of C. G. Jung. Translated by M. D. Eder. London, 1918; New York, 1919. (Jung's contributions, retranslated, in *Collected Works*, 2.)

——. "A Study in the Process of Individuation." In *Collected Works*, 9, i.

——. *Symbols of Transformation*. *Collected Works*, 5. Cf. JUNG, *Psychology of the Unconscious*.

——. "Synchronicity: An Acasual Connecting Principle." In *Collected Works*, 8.

——. "The Transcendent Function." In *Collected Works*, 8.

——. *Two Essays on Analytical Psychology*. *Collected Works*, 7. (2nd edn., 1966.)

KANT, IMMANUEL. *Immanuel Kant's Critique of Pure Reason*. Translated by Norman Kemp Smith. London and New York, 1929.

——. *Logik*. In: *Werke*. Edited by Ernst Cassirer. Berlin, 1912–22. 11 vols. (Vol. 8, pages 325–452.)

KUBIN, ALFRED. *The Other Side*. Translated by Denver Lindley. New York, 1967. (Original: *Die andere Seite*. Munich, 1909.)

LASSWITZ, KURD. *Wirklichkeiten. Beiträge zur Weltverständnis*. Leipzig, 1900.

LEHMANN, ALFRED GEORG LUDWIG. *Die Hauptgesetze des menschlichen Gefühlslebens*. 2nd edn., Leipzig, 1914.

LIPPS, THEODOR. *Leitfaden der Psychologie*. 3rd edn., Leipzig, 1909.

MAEDER, A. *The Dream Problem*. Translated by Frank Mead Hallock and Smith Ely Jelliffe. (Nervous and Mental Disease Monograph Series, 22.) New York, 1916. (Original: "Über das Traumproblem," *Jahrbuch für psychoanalytische und psychopathologische Forschungen* (Vienna), V (1913), 647–86.)

MEYRINK, GUSTAV. *Das grüne Gesicht; eine Roman*. Leipzig, 1916.

NAHLOWSKY, JOSEPH WILHELM. *Das Gefühlsleben in seinen wesentlichsten Erscheinungen und Bezierhungen*. 3rd edn., Leipzig, 1907.

NATORP, PAUL. *Einleitung in die Psychologie nach kritischer Methode*. Freiburg im Breisgau, 1888.

NIETZSCHE, FRIEDRICH. *Thus Spake Zarathustra*. Translated by Thomas Common and revised by Oscar Levy and John L. Beevers. London, 1931.

PRINCE, MORTON. *The Dissociation of a Personality: A Biographical Study in Abnormal Psychology*. New York, 1906.

RIBOT, THÉODULE ARMAND. *Die Persönlichkeit. Pathologisch-psychologische Studien*. Berlin, 1894.

——. *The Psychology of the Emotions*. London, 1897. (Original: *Psychologie der Gefühle*. Altenburg, 1903.)

RIEHL, ALOIS. *Zur Einführung in die Philosophie der Gegenwart*. 4th edn., Leipzig and Berlin, 1913.

SCHOPENHAUER, ARTHUR. *The World as Will and Idea*. Translated by R. B. Haldane and J. Kemp. London, 1883. 3. vols. (Original: *Die Welt als Wille und Vorstellung*. (Sämtliche Werke, ed. by Eduard Grisebach, 6.) Leipzig, 1891.)

SEMON, RICHARD. *The Mneme*. Translated by L. Simon. London, 1921. (Original: *Die Mneme als erhaltendes Prinzip im Wechsel des organischen Geschehens*. Leipzig, 1904.)

SILBERER, HERBERT. *Problems of Mysticism and Its Symbolism*. Translated by Smith Ely Jelliffe. New York, 1917. (Original: *Probleme der Mystik und ihrer Symbolik*. Vienna and Leipzig, 1904.)

STOBAEUS, JOHANNES. *Eclogarum physicarum et ethicorum Libri duo.* Edited by Thomas Gaisford. Oxford, 1850. 2 vols.

SULLY, JAMES. *The Human Mind; a Text-book of Psychology.* London, 1892. 2 vols.

VERAGUTH, OTTO. "Das psycho-galvanische Reflex-Phänomen," *Monatsschrift für Psychologie und Neurologie* (Berlin), XXI (1907), 387–425.

VILLA, GUIDO. *Contemporary Psychology.* Translated by H. Manacorda. London, 1903. (Original: *Einleitung in die Psychologie der Gegenwart.* Leipzig, 1902.)

WULFEN, WILLEM VAN (pseud. of Willem van Vloten). *Der Genussmensch: Ein Cicerone im rücksichtslosen Lebensgenuss.* 3rd edn., Munich, 1911.

WUNDT, WILHELM. *Grundzüge der physiologischen Psychologie.* 5th edn., Leipzig, 1902/3. 3 vols. For translation, see: *Principles of Physiological Psychology.* Translated from the 5th German edn. by Edward Bradford Titchener. London and New York, 1904. (Vol. I only published.)

——. *Logik.* 3rd edn. Stuttgart, 1906–8. 3 vols.

——. *Outlines of Psychology.* Translated by Charles Hubbard Judd. 2nd revised English edn. Leipzig, London and New York, 1902. (Original: *Grundriss der Psychologie.* 5th edn., Leipzig, 1902.)

——. "Was soll uns Kant nicht sein?" In *Philosophische Studien.* Edited by W. Wundt. Leipzig, 1883–1903. 20 vols. (VII, pp, 1ff.)

ZELLER, EDUARD. *A History of Greek Philosophy from the Earliest Period to the Time of Socrates.* Translated by S. F. Alleyne. London, 1881. 2 vols. (Original: *Die Philosophie der Griechen in ihrere Geschichtlichen Entwicklung dargestellt.* Tübingen, 1856–68, 5 vols.)

INDEX

INDEX

THE COLLECTED WORKS OF

C. G. JUNG

The publication of the first complete edition, in English, of the works of C. G. Jung was undertaken by Routledge and Kegan Paul, Ltd., in England and by Bollingen Foundation in the United States. The American edition is number XX in Bollingen Series, which since 1967 has been published by Princeton University Press. The edition contains revised versions of works previously published, such as *Psychology of the Unconscious*, which is now entitled *Symbols of Transformation*; works originally written in English, such as *Psychology and Religion*; works not previously translated, such as *Aion*; and, in general, new translations of virtually all of Professor Jung's writings. Prior to his death, in 1961, the author supervised the textual revision, which in some cases is extensive. Sir Herbert Read (d. 1968), Dr. Michael Fordham, and Dr. Gerhard Adler compose the Editorial Committee; the translator is R. F. C. Hull (except for Volume 2) and William McGuire is executive editor.

The price of the volumes varies according to size; they are sold separately, and may also be obtained on standing order. Several of the volumes are extensively illustrated. Each volume contains an index and in most a bibliography; the final volume will contain a complete bibliography of Professor Jung's writings and a general index to the entire edition.

The Zofingia lectures
Seminar papers: Dream Analysis

See also:

C. G. Jung: Letters

Selected and edited by Gerhard Adler, with Anjela Jaffé. Translation from the German by R. F. C. Hull.
Vol. 1: 1906–1950
Vol. 2: 1951–1961

The Freud-Jung Letters

Edited by William McGuire, translated by Ralph Manheim and R. F. C. Hull

C. G. Jung in Paperback

† Alchemical Studies
† Analytical Psychology: Its Theory and Practice
* Answer to Job: Researchers in the Relation between Psychology and Religion
* Aspects of the Feminine
* Dreams
† Flying Saucers: A Modern Myth of Things Seen in The Sky
† Four Archetypes: Mother, Rebirth, Spirit, Trickster
* Modern Man in Search of a Soul
† Psychological Reflections: An Anthology from the Writings of C. G. Jung
† Psychology and Alchemy
* Psychology and the East
† Psychology and the Occult
* Psychology of the Transference
† On the Nature of the Psyche
* The Spirit in Man, Art and Literature
* Synchronicity: An Acasual Connecting Principle
† The Undiscovered Self: Answers to Questions Raised by the Present World Crisis

By C. G. Jung and C. Kerenyi

† Science of Mythology: Essays on the Myth of the Divine Child and the Mysteries of Eleusis

* Ark paperbacks
† Routledge paperbacks

ARK PAPERBACKS

LES LIAISONS DANGEREUSES

'Even today *Les Liaisons* remain the one French novel that gives us an impression of danger: it seems to require a label on its cover reserving it for external use only.' – Jean Giraudoux

A great sensation at the time of first publication, with readers attempting to identify the real-life originals of the novel's characters, *Les Liaisons Dangereuses* reads as much the most 'modern' of eighteenth-century novels. It shows two experienced 'libertines', planning together to seduce two innocent characters whose lives they thus destroy. A married woman is also seduced and then abandoned as part of the game.

Brilliantly observed and vividly rendered in the letters which make up the novel, the characters take on a life of their own. Laclos lays bare layer after layer of their souls until we know them intimately. The novel is, as Richard Aldington writes in the Introduction, 'a tragic story well told, with a subtlety of psychological analysis not unworthy of a countryman of Stendhal, Flaubert and Balzac.'

PIERRE AMBROISE FRANCOIS CHODERLOS DE LACLOS

Born in Amiens in 1741, Pierre Ambroise Françoise Choderlos de Laclos entered the army at the age of eighteen and spent the next twenty years in various garrison towns without ever seeing battle. In 1779 he was sent to the island of Aix to assist in building a fort, and there wrote Les Liaisons Dangereuses. In 1786 he married Marie-Soulange Duperré and became an exemplary husband and father. He left the army in 1788, entered politics and was twice imprisoned during the Reign of Terror. He returned to the army as a general under Napoleon in 1800, and died at his post in Taranto, Italy, in 1803.

Laclos also wrote a treatise on the education of women and another on Vauban, but it is for *Les Liaisons Dangereuses,* his single masterpiece, that he is remembered.

ARK PAPERBACKS is an imprint of Routledge & Kegan Paul and can be ordered through your usual bookshop.